CHINA DOCTOR
of John Day

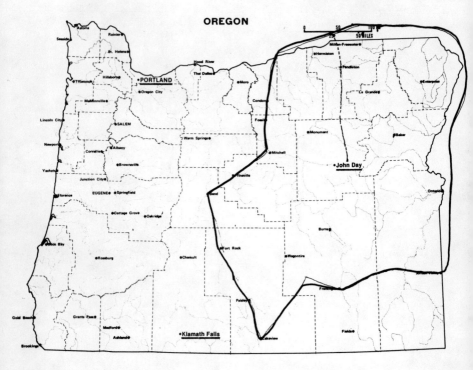

The China Doctor's Medical Territory

CHINA DOCTOR
of John Day

Jeffrey Barlow
and
Christine Richardson

Binford & Mort
Thomas Binford, Publisher

2536 S.E. Eleventh • Portland, Oregon 97202

Dedication

For Lewis A. Barlow, who would have been proud to ride with Buckaroo Sam or Markee Tom.

JGB

For Chester A. Richardson, an Oregon pioneer who sought and found his fortune in Asia.

CAR

China Doctor of John Day
Copyright © 1979 by Binford & Mort, Publishers

Printed in the United States of America
Library of Congress Catalog Card Number: 79-3300
ISBN: 0-8323-0346-1
First Edition 1979

Contents

Introduction................................... *vii*

1. Ing Hay and His Terrible Brew................. 1

2. Kwangtung to John Day 4

3. Chinatown—John Day 9

4. The Partners............................... 34

5. Herbalist and Pulsologist..................... 54

6. The Golden Flower Blooms 71

7. .... and Fades............................. 88

Appendix
Sixty-two Chinese Herbs and Medications 98

Photograph Section *109*

The Authors *118*

Introduction

Ing Hay was an immigrant from China who came to this country as a young man to work as a gold miner, like tens of thousands of his countrymen. Though the Chinese immigrants who went to California to mine are best known to historians and writers of popular fiction, television, and movie scripts, the Chinese miners of Oregon, Washington, and Idaho were relatively more important to the development of the Pacific Northwest than were the Chinese of California.

The Chinese brought not only their traditional medicine with them, but many other skills as well. After the passing of the frontier and the mines, many stayed in the same region and made a lasting contribution to its growth. Ing Hay's partner, Lung On, for example, came to this country in the 1880s as an immigrant, mined gold, gambled, and eventually became a very successful modern businessman and the first automobile dealer in Eastern Oregon.

The lives of Ing Hay and Lung On began in China, but it was in the mining frontier of Eastern Oregon and Washington that they became significant to the historian and to the community of John Day in which they lived. The mining frontier of the area around Eastern Oregon, including parts of Washington and Idaho, was among the last of the American frontiers and was in many ways a typical part of the "Wild West."

The history of Ing Hay and the Chinese community of John Day gives a rewarding and accurate picture of the Chinese immigrant on the American Frontier. Ing Hay, Lung On, and other Chinese immigrants like Markee Tom and Buckaroo Sam were not faceless stereotypical Chinamen. They were remarkable individuals and true pioneers—and most of their contemporaries and heirs to the developing region of Eastern Oregon knew it. Their contribution to the process of building civilized society in the region is remembered and honored there today.

Acknowledgments

This book grew out of our involvement in the project to restore the Kam Wah Chung Building in which Ing Hay, the China Doctor, and his partner, Lung On, lived for so many years. Out of our efforts grew a strong interest in the history of the Chinese community in Eastern Oregon, and we began the research which has culminated in this book.

China Doctor and the entire restoration project could not have been completed without the selfless assistance of many people. We can extend thanks here to only a few of those who gave time, labor and funds that Ing Hay and Lung On and the Chinese immigrants into Eastern Oregon might be remembered. We are grateful to the many students and professionals who assisted us in earlier stages of the project: James Davidson Moss, Kerry Fuse, Dr. Douglas Chen, David Lung, Pat Moss, and our friend, Dr. K'ai-hua Ger, who contributed in a major way to the medical research necessary to the project and the book.

We are also grateful to two of Oregon's leading educational institutions, Lewis and Clark College and the University of Oregon. Both schools gave us time from our work there, funds for travel, and the invaluable assistance of their talented students. We are particularly grateful to our friends on the faculty and staff of Lewis and Clark College who have given us necessary support.

We owe a special debt to the Oregon Historical Society and Chia-lin Chen, who during his association with it paved our

viii

way in the research by translating some of the key documents in the Kam Wah Chung collection. We also recognize the contribution of David Powers of Oregon State Parks, whose always professional attitude did much to help us through the sometimes rocky path of the project.

We are especially grateful to the members of the Kam Wah Chung Commission of John Day, whose members saw the project through to completion; and to Janice J. Justice, curator, Herman and Eliza Oliver Historical Museum, Canyon City, who collected and organized some of the newspaper materials quoted in this work.

We owe a special debt to the members of the Chinese-American communities of Oregon, Washington, and Idaho, who patiently told us of their past experiences as immigrants to the Pacific Northwest. We are also indebted to our typist, June Armstrong Richardson, who unfailingly delivered a better manuscript than we gave her; and to our children, Lewis Jefferson Barlow and Bret Michael Reis, who patiently tolerated their parents' need to write this book.

1.
Ing Hay and His Terrible Brew

The Eastern Oregon winter of 1919-1920 was a hard one. In late December, the temperature had hit twenty-two degrees below in John Day, and a thermometer in Bear Valley had given up and frozen solid at fifty degrees below. In those weather conditions and on the unpacked dirt roads of the area, work and travel in the outdoors was an extreme hardship. So remarkable was it to make a drive of more than twenty or thirty miles that to do so was often reported in the paper, as when the *Blue Mountain Eagle* announced on January 23, 1920: "Ira Mahan drove his Ford over from Burns Friday."

It was inevitable that again this year the flu would strike among the road crew, and it did. These laborers—who were forging the final transportation link between Grant County and Portland—were a hardy and determined breed, many of them former miners. They all knew that modern medicine was helpless before the flu. Medical doctors did not agree on the cause of the disease and had no real treatment except to send the patient to bed and hope for the best. Many of them did not trust doctors, in any event, remembering the quacks who had followed the miners into the gold fields in the nineteenth century, and seeing the failure of doctors to prevent the thousands of deaths in Portland alone in the epidemics of 1918-19.

These laborers did, however, trust the medical wisdom of a member of their own community, Ing Hay, the "China Doctor." Ing Hay, the men knew, was the most famous and capable frontier physician of the area. He served patients from the late nineteenth century to 1948, when he retired. He was a traditional Chinese herbal physician whose practice of medicine was based on an entirely different approach from that of the increasingly laboratory-oriented doctors who were so helpless in the face of the earlier influenza.

Ing Hay was far more successful in treating the ills and injuries of the frontier than were the conventional physicians of his time. Some of his cures were truly remarkable, and although we can verify that they did occur, we cannot always explain his methods. Some of the diseases with which he was so successful continue to defy medical practitioners even today.

When word of the flu got back to Ing Hay and his partner Lung On in John Day, Lung On drove out to the work camps with Hay and his medicines. Ing Hay took along literally gallons of a bitter herbal mixture which he warmed over stoves in the rude shelters of the road crews. Trusting Ing Hay from their own personal experience with him during previous illnesses, or from the wisdom passed down by their fathers, they drank the brew, although it smelled and tasted terrible.

Though many of the men fell ill with the flu, none became bedridden and all continued to work. So, because of the two Chinese and the trust between them and the road crew, in late February, 1920, the goods truck came up the long grade, and with it, the twentieth century came to Grant County, Oregon, in the form of a truckload of potatoes. James D. Fine drove this first truckload over the newly opened highway which now linked Grant County—with its economic center at John Day and its county seat at Canyon City—with Portland. The local paper, the *Blue Mountain Eagle*, fully understood the significance of the truck and gave it a column lead in its issue of Friday, March 5, 1920, observing that "This trip might be considered a little remarkable for this season of the year, and yet it illustrates what will transpire on the completion of the highway when transportation will be made easy."

The link to Portland worked a transformation in Grant County. In the period before the truck's arrival, despite the undeniable progress in the area, and the arrival of the twentieth century right on time in more urban settings like Portland, Grant County was still very much the frontier. It was cut off from the world except by the most arduous effort. In September of 1914, for example, the local paper gravely reported that Mrs. Shelly of John Day was seriously injured in a stagecoach accident on the Long Creek to Canyon City run when the four-horse team got away from the driver on a grade and threw her off the jouncing vehicle. Canyon City, the county seat, was not seriously to consider electric street lights until October of 1917.

Despite the lack of many modern conveniences, the major problem for the people of the county was economic. The long and slow process of transportation so increased the price of the products of Grant County mines, mills, farms, and ranches that people could not find sizable markets in which they could afford to compete. This kept the area an economic and cultural backwater. After the highway was opened, what had been a limited, local market was expanded considerably in the immediate area, and now the way to Portland and maritime transportation lay open as well.

Poor roads had been the main obstacle to that progress, and the folks of Grant County had lobbied industriously to finish the remaining links in the state highway system which were not graded or paved—from Prairie City to John Day and from John Day south and west to Prineville. As the county had watched the progress of the road gang through the mountain passes to the north and southwest, there were many who feared that the flu would halt the highway and spring rains would stop it for another year after funds were exhausted. Thanks largely to Ing Hay and his "terrible brew," the highway was completed on schedule!

2.
Kwangtung to John Day

The new road into the John Day Valley, which Ing Hay and Lung On had helped put through, led not only to Portland but also to China. The portion of the road which led through the canyons west of John Day were parallel to The Dalles Military Road, which had been the major trail from the Columbia River through Eastern Oregon into the gold fields of Idaho in the 1860s. It was by way of this road that both Ing Hay and Lung On had made the last leg of their much earlier journeys from Canton to their ultimate home, John Day. Both men belonged to the first generation of immigrants to enter the gold fields of Eastern Oregon.

Like most of the thousands of Chinese who lived and worked in the American West, the Chinese of John Day came from the southern part of China. Ing Hay, or Doc Hay as he is known to history, was born in the small village of Hsia Pin Li, Toisan County, Kwangtung, in 1862. His family members, like most of the people of that area, were primarily peasants and desperately poor.

In the mid-nineteenth century, when Ing Hay grew to young manhood, the peace and stability necessary for wresting a living from the Chinese soil were lacking. The sources of turmoil were many, but the major problem was simply overpopulation. For several centuries this had increased so rapidly that agricultural production could not keep pace. The smallest fluctuation in the natural cycles of weather caused famines which killed millions.

During this unstable time, foreigners began arriving in Southern China. In the 1860s, the English demanded access to its products and markets. In fact, they purchased so much Chinese tea that they had to find something to sell in China or suffer a great imbalance of trade. Opium was the answer. It was the perfect product for their needs, and it was produced in previously conquered English colonies in India. The Chinese government tried to prevent the opium trade but England was not to be denied. After a series of short and brutal wars around Canton, British opium began to circulate freely throughout China. It became such a scourge that travelers and missionaries spoke of entire villages where so many were in an opium stupor that no crops were planted and no business transacted.

Chinese from South China had been much more accustomed than other Chinese to travel and trade, and one response to famine and war had always been migration. However, because of the importance of the ancestral farms, temples and graves, the entire family rarely left. Then, it was usually the younger sons who went out looking for work or trade abroad.

Sometime in the 1860s or the 1870s—we cannot be certain—Ing Hay's five uncles decided to leave their farm and look for work abroad. According to a relative, Ing Hay's family was among the large number of southern Chinese who opposed the Manchus. This opposition to the ruling elite, coupled with the poor economic situation in China, gave the five Ing brothers ample incentive to flee their homeland in search of fortune elsewhere.

Early in the 1880s, word came back from Ing Hay's uncles that they had found work in the United States and were doing well. By this time the path of emigration was well trodden. Chinese from the south of China had gone out all over the world. There were Chinese in North and South America, Europe, and Africa, but North America was particularly attractive. Because of the great wave of western expansion in both the United States and Canada, the growth of the railways, and the successive gold booms, the need for unskilled labor was great. At least a quarter of a million Chinese took ship from China for the western United States in the late nineteenth and early twentieth centuries.

Among those shipping out were Ing Hay and his father, who

planned to join Ing Hay's uncles, now located in Walla Walla, Washington.

At first, the young men who left China to seek their fortunes abroad always assumed that they would one day return to their homeland. Often they would marry before they left, perhaps start a family, which would then live with their parents, while they sent home money for support. Whether Ing Hay had long since prepared to migrate or simply wished to marry, we do not know, but he did start a family in Toisan County. He soon had a son, Shih-shao, and a daughter, Lien-yung.

It seems certain that Ing and his father arrived in the United States in the year 1883. Ing himself was never specific as to time and place. There are several versions of his arrival, all of which he contributed to. Occasionally he even claimed to have been born in Walla Walla.

The previous year, 1882, had been crucial for Chinese immigrants because in that year the United States passed the Chinese Exclusion Act. Now that the great wave of railway building was tapering off and gold strikes were less frequent, Americans wished to exclude Chinese labor. The Act limited emigration from China to educated intellectuals and merchants.

Because Canada was developing at a somewhat slower pace, it still had much need for cheap labor, and Canadian immigration laws were far less restrictive. But, once in Canada, it was a relatively easy matter to slip across the long, largely unpatrolled border into the Pacific Northwest. An item in the *Grant County News* of Canyon City, December 20, 1888, observed: "It is said that smugglers receive $30 per head for running the Chinese over the border into Washington Territory."

During this period, Port Townsend and Walla Walla were key towns for the migrating Chinese. The former was a major small port with very lax immigration authorities, if any. It also had several large and thriving Chinese businesses and a sizable Chinese community, thus offering a good point of entry for illegal Chinese immigration. It seems possible that Ing Hay and his father entered in just that fashion. Whether they were legal at the time they entered is not really an important question because the rapid series of exclusion acts in the 1880s created confusion and ambiguity for even legal migrants. Nobody could ever be sure that if they had entered legally, they still remained legally. In these circumstances, Ing Hay may have been vague in order to give himself plenty of room for legal maneuver should it ever become necessary.

Walla Walla—where Ing Hay and his father were to join the five brothers—was then a boom town, the center of transportation and communication for the gold fields and mining towns of the northwestern interior of both the United States and Canada. Because of these gold fields and the railway construction projects, it attracted a large population of Chinese immigrants who went out from there as miners, laborers, and merchants. Today all that remains in Walla Walla of a once-booming Chinese community of several thousand are several Chinese restaurants, some prosperous merchants, and Chinese-American professional people. There is a small monument in the local cemetery where approximately a hundred gravestones, many broken and illegible, testify to the contribution of the Chinese in building the town.

In 1885, when Ing Hay and his father finally arrived in Walla Walla, the bloom was off because the gold mines were less productive and other transportation routes had replaced the "Wild Horse Trail," which ran from Walla Walla through the Kootenai up to British Columbia. Nonetheless, there were still several hundred Chinese living there in a highly organized community. Many of those Chinese were surnamed Ing and they cooperated loosely with each other, although they did not regard each other as "real" relatives in the western sense.

While sharing a common name did not make most Chinese really close, it did make some difference. On being introduced for the first time, strangers sharing the same family name often greeted each other with the ritual, "A thousand years ago we were one family." However, the Ings, a smaller family, were especially clannish and tended to stay together in the Pacific Northwest.

Ing Hay and his father remained in Walla Walla for some time, trying a bit of mining and working as unskilled laborers. Then, in 1887, for unknown reasons, the father decided to go back to China. Possibly he had to return to take up his responsibilities as family head. It is also possible that he could not learn English or adapt to western ways. English is one of the most difficult tongues for a foreigner to pick up, and Ing Hay himself never learned more than a broken "pidgin" English in the sixty or so years he was to live in the Pacific Northwest.

A unique historical document, a letter later written to Ing Hay by his father, translated by Chia-lin Chen, and now in the possession of the Oregon Historical Society, tells us what happened between the two when Ing Hay saw his father off for China. Ing Hay said to his father, "Let the old go back home and rest. Let the young seek their fortune abroad." This was to be Ing Hay's last real contact with his family, for he was never to return to China nor keep in close touch by mail.

Ing Hay's uncles remained in Walla Walla, where some of them are buried today, but Ing Hay himself left for John Day, Oregon, in 1887, the same year his father returned to China. He was then only twenty-five years old and still something of a greenhorn, speaking only broken English but setting out bravely into the unknown to seek his fortune. We have a picture of him from this time which shows an unusually handsome Chinese youth, wearing a queue and traditional clothing with a remarkably confident air.

3.
Chinatown—John Day

Canyon City was the major town in Eastern Oregon when Ing Hay arrived in 1887. It had its origins in the accidental discovery of gold in Canyon Creek. A party of miners were en route to the boom at the Florence mines in Idaho in June of 1862 when they camped for the evening beside the creek. Unable to rest without first checking the creek bottom, one of the men brought up a pan full of "color" and the gold boom came to Eastern Oregon. News went out and a thirty-two-wagon train of Californians, also on their way to Idaho, diverted and settled in the area that July. Several of them opened up a small store, Becker and Zimmerman's, and Canyon City had its beginning.

It was formally established one year later when it had some fifteen hundred inhabitants. As the town grew more established and refined, another town grew up on the creek below it. Variously called "Other Town," "Tiger Town," and "Lower Town," this community served primarily as the "other side of the tracks" for the thriving metropolis of Canyon City. In the long run, however, "Lower Town," which was to become "John Day"—named for the nearby river— was better placed. Canyon City was too far up the canyon for which it was named, and the main roads developed in such a way as to bypass it in favor of John Day.

When Ing Hay arrived at John Day, Canyon City was still the area's center. At John Day, however, there was a thriving Chinatown of five to six hundred inhabitants. The origins of the John Day Chinatown are closely tied to the development of gold mining in the area.

While some significant mining strikes had been made in Eastern Oregon in 1860-62, the development of the road brought thousands of miners into the region and Canyon City came to be their major center. Strikes made again in British Columbia, and in the Caribou and Kootenai areas in the period from 1861 to 1863, also attracted many along the new road in 1864.

The dominant image of the gold miner in contemporary America is probably the single prospector with his "jenny" and gold pan, immortalized by television commercials and inaccurate western movies. That sort of prospector was limited; he could only pan "placer" gold, which had been deposited in small rivers and creeks over the millennia as it eroded from larger deposits higher in the mountains and hills. The placer prospector was critical in the early days of the 1848 gold rush in California, and he continues to be found to the present, because of the small amount of capital investment necessary to that sort of search.

In the 1860 gold strikes in Idaho and Oregon, the first discoveries were made by the lone wolf placer miners, but real exploitation required either deep vein mining or hydraulic mining. The technology of deep-vein mining was expensive and the ore difficult to ship, so it had to wait until transportation improved in the 1890s. At that time, mining became a long-term, serious business, which usually excluded the individual entrepreneur who had neither the capital nor the knowledge.

The alternative to placer mining and deep-vein mining was the hydraulic method. There is a similarity here to placer mining in that both methods seek alluvial gold—gold deposited in stream beds. The hydraulic miner was aware that the beds of ancient streams were as rich or richer than the easily-reached beds of live rivers and streams, and he devised an ingenious method to get at such beds, often covered by many feet of more recent geological deposits. The hydraulic miner used streams high in the hills above his site, or pumped water up to great heights, and then released it under tremendous pressure through huge hoses which were capable of moving tons of soil very quickly.

Hydraulic mining was an expensive business, and the men who undertook it were as much hardheaded businessmen as footloose prospectors. A method similar in expense and complexity was the operation of huge dredges which picked up and screened the bottoms of small rivers and large creeks. At a certain point the return from these methods became inadequate and the engineers and their machinery moved on.

Chinese miners had been important at all stages of this process. They came in leading burros and carrying gold pans, just as did the white placer miners, but they also stayed and, as hired laborers, did the backbreaking work of operating the large hydraulic nozzles and picking through the gravel exposed by the dredges. They were often favored by the large mining companies for the same reason that the large railway firms hired them—they worked quite cheaply and were both disciplined and hard working. Furthermore, they had little legal protection under the law, were easily cheated, and unlikely to resort to violence if they were. One still hears stories from various parts of the Northwest about mines where Chinese labor gangs were simply entombed with powder blasts rather than paid off when the mines closed.

By the 1870s, when the easy riches of the placer mining process and the quick returns from the hydraulic and the dredge operations were exhausted, the Chinese miner came into his own. The remaining method of mining was the patient, difficult process of panning the great gravel banks left by the high-pressure hoses and the dredges. Because this work was laborious and did not offer quick returns, many white miners tended not to take it up. They quickly sold or leased their claims to Chinese miners.

When the Chinese miners began to work, however, they met bitter resentment from some of the whites of the area. There was, of course, nothing new about such attitudes. Whites and Chinese had frequently clashed in the gold fields of California. As the gold fields of Washington, Oregon, and Idaho brought

Chinese to the Pacific Northwest, anti-Chinese sentiment soon followed.

Anti-Chinese prejudices not only exposed the Chinese miner to irrational acts of racial violence but often denied him the protection of the law. Claim jumping was a particular problem for the Chinese, who often bought supposedly worked-out claims from one of a series of whites who had owned them. If the Chinese seemed successful, whites were prone to move back in, asserting a prior claim to the land or, in extreme cases, simply murdering the Chinese and taking the accumulated gold and the land.

There are several examples of claim jumping from 1886 which almost seem to receive the approval of the white press, as illustrated in this story in the *Grant County News*, November 1886: "Some of the 'Northfork Boys' who jumped the Chinamen's claim last spring have made their fortunes and retired from business; anyway they have gone." A more violent incident was noted in the same paper, July 7, 1887: "The Chinese, in San Francisco, have sent out detectives up into Idaho, to ferret out, if possible, the guilty parties who murdered a gang of Chinese miners on Snake River lately."

Ing Hay arrived in Canyon City area just after one such incident. When the Chinese had come to dominate mining there in the 1870s, they had built a "Chinatown," an area of Chinese stores and small shacks adjoining Canyon City. There were a series of fires in the area, and it seemed likely that tension between disgruntled whites and Chinese was at least partially responsible for both the frequency of the fires and the often lackadaisical response of the white-controlled fire-fighting apparatus. Finally, in February of 1885, the Chinatown, which may have had close to a thousand inhabitants, burned completely.

Local authorities would not allow the Chinese to rebuild, so they moved down the creek several miles to "Lower Town," or "Other Town," the community that would become John Day. The Chinatown of John Day was, in fact, the most important part of the little community when it began in 1885. It was centered on a remarkable building which still stands—now the Kam Wah Chung and Co. Museum, dedicated to the memory of Ing Hay and the contribution of the Chinese to the area's development.

The building was, in 1885, basically a square structure perhaps thirty feet on each side. It was made of the hard stone native to the area, quarried a few miles from the spot. The walls were several feet thick, and it was pierced only by small windows covered by steel shutters outside and wooden ones inside. The best evidence indicates the building was constructed sometime in the 1860s, when it was probably a trading post and minor fortification on The Dalles Military Road. Construction of the building suggests that it was originally built by Chinese, for it is in a style vaguely reminiscent of the farmhouses of the south China plain. We do know that the building was in existence well in advance of 1879, because a lease from that year still exists. It was owned by a Chinese or a company of Chinese in 1885 when the community was swelled with the refugees from the Canyon City fire. Basically a store which sold the necessities of daily life on the frontier, its size and solid structure suggest that even in 1885 it must have been the physical and economic center of the new Chinatown which grew up around it.

Many of the Chinese from Canyon City, though, chose not to rebuild in that area but moved back into Walla Walla or farther east into Sand Point or Boise, Idaho, both of which had thriving Chinatowns. About five to six hundred people did move down the creek to John Day, however, and the new Chinatown soon had three well-established stores, a temple or "joss house," communal ponds where fish and ducks were raised, large vegetable gardens, a laundry, and many small shacks and shanties.

It was to this thriving community of his fellow Chinese immigrants that Ing Hay came in 1887. He was soon approached by the remarkable man who would be his lifelong friend and business partner, Lung On, or "Leon," as he was eventually to be called. Lung On had come to the United States in 1882, ahead of Ing Hay, and had landed at San Francisco. He arrived in Canyon City itself in 1887, just before Ing Hay. Shortly after Ing Hay arrived, Lung On approached him with a business proposition: the two should become the major partners in a company to be operated out of the little Chinatown's most impressive structure, the stone-walled Kam Wah Chung and Co. building.

It is clear what attracted Lung On to Ing Hay. The great majority of Chinese miners in the area were from Toisan County in Kwangtung, around Canton. Ing Hay, too, was from Toisan and spoke their dialect, which was slightly different from Lung On's own. As place of origin back in Kwangtung was extremely important to the Chinese—who did their best to reproduce the familiar institutions from the old country here in the new—a partner from Toisan guaranteed the store a considerable advantage. Ing Hay had another attraction as well: many of the Chinese in the region were themselves Ings by family name and thus regarded themselves as relations of all other Ings.

Ing Hay's greatest attraction for Lung On, however, was probably that he had some training in classical Chinese medicine and intended to practice in the mining frontier as a traditional Chinese herbal doctor, a "China doctor" as they were known to the white community. As noted already, the dangers of the labor in an isolated mining camp were great and frequently disastrous. This was especially true for Chinese working far from their supportive families and native communities. For a Chinese miner to be crippled or even badly injured was often as fatal as being killed outright; the Chinese community could not afford to keep cripples or convalescents about who could not work.

Often such unfortunates simply committed suicide with the full knowledge and support of the entire community. An example of several such suicides is contained in an interview in the possession of the Jacksonville Museum at Jacksonville,

Oregon. The narrator is an old-timer from the region, Glen Simpson. Mr. Simpson told of several accidents involving Chinese laborers and the "black pill," during the 1880s when the railways were going through the Siskiyou Mountains. Typical incidents were told to him by Dr. F. S. Parsons of Ashland. A young doctor had come out from the East as his assistant:

Up on the Siskiyous in '87 they had an explosion in a tunnel and there were five Chinamen, two killed outright and three were badly maimed, and so this young doctor, he undertook to do surgery on the three who was left and then he came back to town to report to Dr. Parsons. Dr. Parsons, he caught him at the Alhambra saloon and Dr. Parsons says, "You see that livery stable across the street? Well, go over there and get you a fresh team of horses and get back up that hill as fast as you can." When the young doctor got back to the tunnel on the Siskiyous, there was just five graves on the side of the hill and no Chinaman in sight. That was the first time that I knew about the black pills—that they put anybody that was maimed out of the way.

The second time was when a nurse told me of the experience right in the Granite City Hospital in Ashland where one Chinaman had part of a foot off and they had infection in it, but they had cured it up and thought that it would be well and that the Chinaman could go home the next day. And the Chinaman, he said, "No, me no go home, me die today." But the nurse, she couldn't understand that, and the Chinaman had a five dollar bill and he tried to give it to the nurse. The nurse said she wouldn't take it, so later on here comes a group of Chinamen with a bowl of soup for the boy. So, in giving the soup to him, why, evidently they slipped the black pills to this Chinaman because thirty minutes after, or less, after the Chinaman left, he was dead and gone. All the doctors thought they had done a wonderful job of surgery on this Chinaman.

The third time was .... they finally made me leave the hospital and we came back to town and I put away the ambulance and came back over to the city jail to turn in the key.

Why, I looked across the plaza and here was Mr. Scott, the undertaker, with the wagon going toward the hospital. So, I went in and asked Mr. McNab if he had heard anything from the Chinaman. He said no, and I said there goes Doc—you'd better call up. So he called up the hospital and sure enough the Chinaman died before we ever got back to town. And that was a case where I'd seen the Chinaman half an hour ago as he swallowed the pill.

The "black pill" was, of course, opium. An overdose of opium was a traditional means of suicide for the Chinese. From these examples, one can see at the same time the supportive nature of Chinese society and its limitations. The Chinese could not support unproductive members of the community in the hostile frontier environment. Because invalids could not be returned home to their families because of the expense, the unlucky laborer had no choice but quietly to commit suicide, perhaps with the help of his friends.

For a community like this, a doctor of their own people was a wonderful advantage. As we shall point out later, the "China Doctor, he would never have had a severe infection, would not and experience, was in many ways far superior to the American physician of the period. To name one example which we shall later go into detail, the herbal physician had far better cures for blood poisoning and infection than did western science at that time. Had the injured Chinese laborer had access to a China Doctor, he would never have had a several infection, would not have lost part of his foot, would not have become a liability to his community—and would consequently have lived.

Lung On, then, recognized in Ing Hay—"Doc Hay"—a major asset to the frontier Chinese miners and laborers, a man with medical training who was also related to many of them. It is no wonder that Lung On asked the younger man to go into partnership.

Doc Hay, in turn, was probably drawn to Lung On for the reason that other people were drawn to him during his entire life. Lung On was an exceptionally personable man with a great deal of confidence and courage. Of his many fine qualities perhaps the most exceptional was his intelligence. Several people said of him, in interviews conducted for this book, that he was "the smartest man I ever knew." Considering Lung On's origins as a Chinese immigrant, such remarks are remarkable testimony indeed, for many people find it less easy to perceive intelligence or other good qualities in a person of another race.

Lung On's intellectual capabilities were bicultural; he was an accomplished person by both Chinese and American standards. He was raised as a young scholar and was familiar with the Chinese Confucian classics, a very esoteric and demanding body of documents. He could write in the language of the texts, classical Chinese, a language quite different from the language spoken by peasants. To be conversant with the classics and to be able to write in the classical language were the most impressive of accomplishments from a Chinese perspective.

Lung On had, however, another remarkable ability: he could speak fluent English and communicate with Americans on their own terms rather than in the demeaning pidgin, which Americans found so comical. Lung On had entered the country only in 1882 and we know he spoke good English by 1887. Obviously he was quick to learn. We do not know whether he attended school in this country or not. Some few hardy souls did enter school here and worked their way up quickly through the American educational system, but most were so much older that they found it difficult to attend school with American children. Too, the parents of many children resented adult "Mongolian" males attending school with their young daughters. Such resentment was a recurrent factor in West Coast anti-Oriental sentiment in the late nineteenth century.

Several of the older Chinese interviewed had gone to public schools only briefly and then had found a tutor with whom they could study. The Salvation Army and other public aid societies seem to have been a frequent source for such tutors. Lung On may have taken this path; however, it seems entirely possible that he was self taught. When the artifacts of the Kam Wah Chung building were cleaned and classified in the summers of 1976 and 1977, a number of well-read English language books which belonged to Lung On were found. The books included many nineteenth century classics, such as the works of Charles Dickens and Guy de Maupassant. There were also several worn-out nineteenth century editions of various Chinese-English dictionaries and phrase books.

The nineteenth century prized the attributes of education in a way that we do not today. Although education is regarded as the surest ladder to upward mobility, few take pride in their penmanship or writing style. Lung On's writing was highly prized by Chinese, who asked him to write letters, to draft temple documents, and to prepare specimens of calligraphy for their walls. The white community thought so highly of his writing that the freight manager in nearby Prairie City framed an order which Lung On sent him and placed it up on the wall of the depot.

Lung On's intellectual abilities were matched by his sense of adventure. Thus far, in describing Lung On, one might have been listing the qualities of mind of a classical Chinese scholar. However, Lung On was not only an intellectual but a man of action as well. His venturesome nature is first evidenced by the fact that he emigrated when it is clear that he could have well afforded to remain in China.

Lung On's love of adventure was so well developed as to border on recklessness. Perhaps his penchant for gambling best reveals that side of his nature. Lung On loved to gamble, would play Chinese or American card games, mah-jong, dominoes, fan-tan, and other such games. In the early period before the two partners grew prosperous, his gambling was occasionally a serious problem. Doc Hay mentioned in 1887, in a letter to a Chinese friend, that Lung On had lost a large part of the company's funds while gambling with Americans in Portland and Baker. Hay would get angry with Lung On, according to witnesses, because he thought that Lung On spent too much time with women and too much time away from the business with his race horses. Whether Lung On grew more cautious or simply became more skilled, we do not know, but unlike many Chinese who shared his vice, he died wealthy.

In interviewing older Chinese, we found that several mentioned the great scourge of gambling and saw it as far more serious than opium as an obstacle to success for Chinese immigrants. One Chinese said that the reason he had prospered while other Chinese had failed was that he did not gamble.

As Lung On grew older, his gambling focused upon horse racing. We know that he took frequent trips to Portland and San Francisco and we assume that at least part of his reason was to visit the metropolitan tracks. In John Day he kept a race horse and hired a professional trainer and a jockey for it. He ran the horse with some success for several years before his death. To the Chinese, traditionally, a horse was a bothersome and expensive animal. Other than those owned by foreigners, the horse was a rare animal in the south of China. It ate too much to keep. Besides, the more patient and dependable water buffalo was a much better draft animal. It was not simply a matter of money, either; the Chinese gentry associated the horse with war and with uncouth soldiers more than with wealth and status. For Lung On to have taken up racing and riding is a measure of the degree to which he became an American.

Doc Hay saw in Lung On, then, not only a personable and exceptionally learned and intelligent man but also a Chinese who had made an unusually thorough and rapid adaptation to American ways. We can easily picture Hay and Lung On when they met. Hay still wore his queue and his Chinese clothes. He was newly arrived from the large and traditional Chinese community in Walla Walla. Lung On probably rode up to meet Ing Hay on his own horse, wearing rough cowboy dress, perhaps even carrying one of the many six-guns which were later found in the Kam Wah Chung Building. He spoke colloquial English and could discourse knowingly on the strange ways of the barbarian-Americans. It is no wonder that the two took so readily to each other and went together to purchase the Kam Wah Chung and Co. Building. It was to be their home from then on.

We can only speculate about how they raised the funds to establish the business. It seems probable that Lung On had passed some time in the gold fields of Idaho, for he had contacts there. We also assume that perhaps he mined less than he gambled with those who did mine. We know that he was an inveterate and usually successful gambler and that he frequently had the restraint to invest his winnings. Perhaps his share was a gold poke he had saved or money he had won at fan-tan, cards, or horse racing.

We believe that Ing Hay raised his money from the Ing family, which doubtless, like other Chinese clans, had a revolving credit association. A credit association was a pool of funds, derived sometimes from revenue from clan lands and investment, but primarily from numerous small contributions of family members. The clan association of elders would meet and vote as to how best to allocate the funds. Often these funds would be lent at considerable interest to family members who seemed to have sound plans for investing them. After a year or two, the loan, plus interest, would be called in and the money then re-allocated to another chosen individual.

There was another partner in the new enterprise, but he is lost to history, except for his name which appears in a notice in the *Grant County News* of September 27, 1888, when the new store was formally opened: "Ye Nem, Hay Ak [Ing Hay], and Lung On have been appointed receivers of the entire business of the Kam Wah Chung and Co. at John Day." Ye Nem may have been another old-timer in the country who soon sold out his share of the partnership to Lung On and Ing Hay.

Certainly Doc Hay must have had little trouble persuading the Ing family to advance him his share of the purchase price of the business. The building was the most solid construction in the entire area; indeed, it is the only building from the 1860s standing in the region. It was also a valuable asset to the community as a whole because it could be a useful weapon in the constant battle with the U.S. Customs and Immigration Service. After 1882 it was impossible for most classes of Chinese to migrate legally to the United States. Several exceptions were made, however, most conspicuously "merchants." Whether Lung On had already been serving as a sponsor for others or whether he began with the purchase of the building in 1887-88, he soon became the go-between for the Chinese and U.S. Customs.

The Kam Wah Chung and Co. documents include a series of letters to Lung On from Chinese in Seattle and Portland seeking guidance through the intricacies of Customs and Immigration. The "Wooden House," the detention center at every large American port where immigrants were screened and housed until permitted to enter, was a terrifying obstacle to Chinese. The problems of language interpretation, the differences in the two cultures—the American one very legalistic and formal, the Chinese one run more by custom and usage— made it very difficult for even the best prepared to enter the country.

There is one case from 1906 when a Chinese named Ing Kwang-jin succeeded in passing through the Wooden House in Seattle after a delay of eight weeks, during which time the Kam Wah Chung and Co. partners wrote several letters affirming that he was a partner in the store. Whether this was true or a useful fiction is not known, but it illustrates the advantage to the Ing clan of investing in the business through Doc Hay.

There is substantial evidence that Lung On also supplied false papers and documents to Chinese wishing to enter the United States. After 1882, Chinese who could prove they had relatives in the country or had been in residence previously or were merchants or students had the best chance. We have a letter asking for a birth certificate or a business visa for a Chinese living in the Philippines who wished to immigrate to this country. We assume that such assistance did not come cheaply and that getting illegals through immigration should be regarded as part of Lung On's business empire.

In later years, Lung On had a personal friendship with a U.S. Customs officer in Portland and frequently wrote to and visited with him. Whether the man was merely one of Lung On's wide circle of friends we do not know, but we assume that he was quite useful to Lung On upon occasion, whatever the basis of their relationship. There is little doubt that the combined talents of Lung On and Doc Hay resulted in a pleasant and prosperous relationship.

Once they had purchased the building and had begun to run it, the two found themselves at the center of life in the area's extended Chinese community. During 1887 and 1888, a struggle was going on for control of that community. Although there were abundant signs of the conflict in the newspapers of the period, its true dimensions escaped the notice of surrounding whites. Had they been more aware, the whites would doubtless have announced the outbreak of a "Tong War" of the sort waged in Weaverville, California, in 1854 for similar reasons.

The struggle reflected loyalties and conflicts imported from the homeland. Basically it revolved around the county of origin in Kwangtung Province, which centered upon the City of Canton. The counties there were divided between two different dialects of Chinese and loosely affiliated into two groups of distinct associations (hui kuan in Chinese), each representing a dialect group. One group, the Sam Yup Association, had earlier been dominant in the California gold fields because its members had been more numerous among early migrants. As time went on, more members of the second group, the Sze Yup Association, began to migrate.

It happened that the Sze Yup Association included migrants from Toisan and Hsin-hui, Doc Hay's and Lung On's home counties, respectively. This threw the two men into the same association; otherwise it is unlikely they would ever have become friends. As the gold strikes began in Idaho and eastern Oregon, the conflict between the two groups followed their members into the Pacific Northwest. Some authorities have argued that the Sze Yup underwent several different name changes through the 1850s and 1860s, but the Chinese of eastern Oregon continued to refer to Sze Yup and Sam Yup, which really only meant "three counties" and "four counties," referring to the grouping of home counties back in Kwangtung.

In addition to the district associations, there were many other highly organized groups in the Chinese community, such as family associations, temple groups, and various temporary self-help groups such as revolving credit societies. The most noted among these organizations were, of course, the shadowy and much-romanticized tongs. Tong associations often grew up when the community was dominated by a small group of families or district associations which jealously tried to exclude newcomers or less well-connected Chinese from power and status. The tongs provided convenient organizations which could contest with more well-established organizations. Members of the tongs were often also more willing to venture into organized vice and corruption, which those with more to lose might avoid. Struggles between rival groups in the Chinese community, whatever their actual nature, immediately became "tong wars" in the popular white press.

All of the many groups in the Chinese community were inherently competitive, as they usually grew up in a time of turmoil or declining resources. This was especially true in the United States, where the community was detached from its traditional institutions and could not rely upon the often capricious American courts. For a Chinese to be deprived of the support of his family or other associations was thus a real disaster; it meant he was totally alone, perhaps for the first time in his life. We can very occasionally gain flashes of insight into the tightly held secrets of the Chinese community as in this article from the *Grant County News*, Canyon City, December 4, 1890:

The police of Seattle have a troublesome Chinaman on their hands. Quan Toy, aged 40, has been cast off by all his countrymen because of some secret reason and was begging on the street when he was arrested for vagrancy. He served fifteen days in jail and when released refused to go. He says that he cannot live with Chinamen anywhere and that no white person will employ him, but the police are unable to make him tell the reason.

The white community was never quite sure what was going on in the Chinatowns; it did not even indeed understand the nature of the varying Chinese organizations. This excerpt from the *Grant County News* of July 3, 1884, gives insight into one of these organizations:

Col. J. Drew Gray, a correspondent of the London Telegraph . . . furnishes interesting information about the Chinese secret society known as the White Lily . . . .

The White Lily society exercises omnipotent power wherever the Chinese can be found. Its agents are everywhere where its slaves are at work, and there is no escape whatever from its vengeance when offended. No Chinaman can disobey its commands and live, for its officers are continually passing from place to place levying taxes and punishing violations of its rules.

The "Six Companies," as called in California, are branches of the White Lily. It is a secret league into which no European or American has ever entered. It defies all laws except its own . . . . it has never been known to take the life of an American or Englishman.

Although the Triad or Hung Society did have considerable influence over Chinese migrants in many communities in North and South America, there was no organization remotely resembling the "White Lily Society" of Colonel Gray's report. Readers of the day doubtless breathed a sigh of relief that the society had never killed an American or an Englishman, but still, such reports merely increased the suspicion directed by the Chinese.

The Sze Yup group, to which Ing Hay and Lung On belonged, seemed to have settled into Canyon City where it was more dominant. The Sam Yup had moved up with the miners from Jacksonville and settled in "Lower Town" or John Day. Lung On, by virtue of his intellect and force of personality, seems to have become the leader of the Sze Yup. Fragmentary evidence suggests that a Chinese named Kit Lee headed the rival Sam Yup.

The issues that divided the two groups were complex. Not only were they traditional rivals in the old country, but such groups were essential to community life among Chinese in the United States, where they served both political and economic functions. Each group was represented by its temples, credit associations, stores, and shops. The example given above in which Lung On used the Kam Wah Chung and Co. name to help immigrants into the area shows the importance of such institutions. Lung On undoubtedly helped Sze Yup migrants primarily, as they would have been much more likely to have had the necessary introductions to him.

The balance between the two groups was probably always very delicate, but the Canyon City Chinatown fire of 1886 provoked an open struggle. After the fire, hundreds of Sze Yup Association members moved into John Day Chinatown, swamping the smaller and older Sam Yup group.

Similar conflicts often became very violent as each association called on affiliated tongs and hired "highbinders"— mercenary gunmen who were known as "hatchetmen" to the white newspapers. On record are several such wars, which involved hundreds of heavily armed "soldiers" from the district associations or secret societies.

The violence at John Day was on a lesser scale, but it did upon occasion come to the notice of the white press, as in this story from the *Grant County News*, September 2, 1886:

> The two different factions in Chinatown, John Day, came near having a bloody engagement Monday night. All day Tuesday the weaker party was engaged in washing and other pastimes which looks as though they were going to emigrate to a more peaceful clime.

True to the pattern found in other similar conflicts, the Chinese of John Day found American law a useful net in which to entangle their rivals. One example of this tactic ended in tragedy. It began in July of 1886. One Ung Ah Fong was arrested after another Chinese accused him of stealing a purse in a gambling den. Ah Fong was jailed for several weeks. We do not know for certain which society he belonged to, but believe it to have been the Sam Yup. After spending several weeks in jail, Ah Fong hanged himself and left the following note, reprinted in the *Grant County News*, August 5, 1886:

> N. W. Gow, Ung Ah Toy, Kit Lee and other friends: My life is a burden. I was born of good and respectable parents, and not accustomed to confinement in a common prison made for the purpose of holding common criminals. I am disgusted with American law as interpreted by the courts, as I believe the same is a violation of the Burlingame Treaty [between China and America] and should be suppressed. Death loves a shining mark. I am ready to meet Joss. Good bye. Plant me deep. Ung Ah Fong.

As the article goes on to note, the Gow mentioned in the suicide note remarked: "He was a good boy but they put up a job on him." An article from August 12, 1886, notes:

> The Chinese in John Day have been on the warpath lately. Since Ah Fong hung himself the company to which he belonged accused the other company of being indirectly responsible for his death, and they are determined to annihilate the whole gang. The defensive party hired some white men to defend them and peace now reigns in the camp.

Kit Lee seems to have been heavily embroiled in the troubles from the beginning. His name turns up in legal notices several times during the period after he brought suit against other Chinese, probably as part of the Sze Yup-Sam Yup fight. In September, following the Ah Fong case, Kit Lee was beaten up by a white, possibly at the instigation of the rival group, which we assume to have been Ing Hay's and Lung On's Sze Yup.

Another death followed in February of 1887 when a Chinese was found frozen. Then, in late February, Kit Lee himself died in Portland of unstated causes. The *Grant County News* article of March 3, 1887, observed: "Kit was boss of one of the Chinese companies or combinations . . . ." This evidence is no better than circumstantial, but it seems very possible that Kit was the head of the failing Sam Yup group.

The violent incidents mentioned here are probably the least important part of the struggle for control of John Day. Undoubtedly the most decisive weapons were the time-honored Chinese concepts of economic power, social status, etiquette, and the all-embracing network of reciprocal obligation. Slowly the Sze Yup prospered; Lung On arrived and took control of it; Ing Hay came, and the older group's enterprises withered. They soon left entirely, leaving the field to Lung On and Ing Hay and their Sze Yup friends.

The Kam Wah Chung Building operated by Lung On and Ing Hay came to be the center of the Chinese community in Eastern Oregon. The building served many purposes for both the Chinese and white communities, but the economic survival of the building depended initially upon its success as a store in which were sold bulk lots and individual items of daily-use products. Some of the clientele were whites from the area who found the store convenient and would drop in for tobacco or canned goods. The Chinese depended on the store as almost the sole importer of Chinese foods, books, clothing, gambling equipment, firecrackers, religious articles like incense and paper for ceremonial purposes, and other sundries.

Lung On and Doc Hay brought with them the accumulated business experience and practices of the Chinese merchant. By today's standards, some of these practices seem very strange; some even run counter to what we now regard as good business procedure. It was common, for example, for many Chinese businesses to sell products for less than they had actually paid for them.

The problem facing all such enterprises was essentially to generate capital as quickly as possible because capital was hard to come by. It is probable that between Lung On's resources and those of the Ing family, the two men had little more to begin with that the purchase price of the building and its goods. They could, however, get credit from both Chinese and white wholesalers and would sell their merchandise very cheaply in order to convert it rapidly into hard money, which had much more leverage in a capital-scarce frontier environment than equivalent amounts of credit. With the capital they could then get further lines of credit, and by carefully paying off debts at the last possible minute, soon stock an entire line of goods with very little actual investment.

If successful, such an approach permitted a business to gain a firm footing with little investment. If, however, business were slow, a firm might collapse suddenly, leaving behind a confused morass of conflicting claims. Failures among small Chinese firms in John Day were quite common, especially after the gold mines began to fail in the 1880s and 1890s. Ing Hay and Lung On were sometimes very slow to pay their debts; some white firms dunned them repeatedly for years before receiving satisfaction. What was by white standards unethical, or at least sloppy business practice, was by Chinese criteria, mere common sense and custom.

Initially the store's mainstay was the sale of case-lot items and bulk goods since there were still many miners in the surrounding area as well as ranchers and sheepmen. Such isolated individuals would come out of the hills periodically to stock up on necessities—flour, bacon, traps, tools, weapons, and ammunition—then return to their solitary existence for several more months.

The Kam Wah Chung and Co. store also served as a sort of hiring hall for Chinese labor. Although mining had faltered and by 1900 had ended almost completely (save for the solitary figures who still tramped the hills, more committed to a style of life than to a way of making a living) there was still a demand for Chinese labor. As mining waned, ranching and farming and eventually logging began. The immigrants from Toisan were fortunate in that their county had a long tradition of wood-working crafts. A rancher wanting a skilled carpenter or a cook or sheepman, or a cowboy, could go to the Kam Wah Chung, where Lung On would soon find a reliable hand. His ability to speak good English made Lung On the intermediary between the Chinese and white communities, and like Cha-li Tong in Walla Walla, he became a very important figure.

One of the functions of major importance carried on in the Kam Wah Chung was that it served as a sort of post office for the Chinese community. Most Chinese, unlike Lung On and Doc Hay, still regarded themselves as temporary sojourners who looked forward to making enough money to return to China, and they kept in close touch with their ancestral homes and families.

Lung On, as mentioned earlier, was valued for his beautiful calligraphy and elegant style, and illiterate and semi-literate Chinese would pay him a small sum to write letters home. Some of these letters, for one reason or another, were never mailed—or perhaps they are copies of letters which were mailed. Letters coming in from China were sometimes undeliv-erable, and these letters also remained in the building, pro-viding unparalleled insights into the men who lived there and into conditions in their homeland.

The Kam Wah Chung and Co. store also came to be an in-tegral part of the religious life of the Chinese mining commu-nity. On the back wall of the room where Lung On sold dry goods and notions, there was a deep box about three feet by two feet fixed to the wall at about eye level, with the opening toward the viewer. The box had been converted to an altar and was hung with expensive brocade curtains imported from China. On another smaller box within the open outer case was a small seated image from popular Buddhist religion.

Buddhism has as many or more varieties and sects than does Christianity, ranging from deeply philosophical schools which, strictly defined, are not religious at all, to "popular" sects which teach a very colorful religion full of ghosts, demons, beneficent spirits, good-luck charms and amulets, fortune-telling, and noisy public ceremonies. The shrine in the Kam Wah Chung was of this last type. The small "Buddha" or god-figure came all the way from China and was no doubt lovingly cared for until it eventually was installed in the building and Doc Hay became its chief priest. Unfortunately the figure was stolen in the 1950s when the building stood empty, and we cannot be sure of the exact identity of the god. Since popular Buddhism has numerous gods and spirits, the figure could have represented any of dozens of common ones.

According to the many witnesses we have interviewed, Doc Hay was a very religious man. The small altar was carefully tended and daily had offerings placed before it of the "Three Precious Things"—wine, fruit and incense. It is interesting to note that several dried grapefruit were found before the altar when the building was opened prior to restoration; the Chinese introduced the culture of grapefruit to this country.

The altar served many functions for the Chinese. It was a small church in the same sense as a Christian church, where the worshippers could commune with those supernatural forces and eternal values with which the Christian's worship puts him in touch. The shrine was also a means of petitioning the god to grant favors. One can imagine that since many of Doc Hay's visitors were medical patients, the Buddha figure heard numerous petitions for good health. Doubtless other major concerns revolved around loved ones back home in China, some of whom were probably praying before a similar shrine for the support and good fortune of relatives in the gold fields of the Pacific Northwest.

The shrine also served a major purpose in divination and fortunetelling. There were a number of ways in which the petitioner or the priest, Ing Hay, could consult the Buddha figure about future events or ask its advice on personal and business problems. Before this shrine there still remain several sets of divining blocks: two pieces of wood, cut and carved from a single piece of rosewood which was originally cylindrical in shape. Cutting the piece in two, down the main axis, gave each half a flat side and a rounded side. The petitioner held the two pieces together as a cylinder before the god while he framed his question, then allowed the pieces to drop gently upon the floor in front of the altar. If both pieces landed flat side up, that was a negative answer to the question asked; if both rounded sides came up, it was a positive response; and if one of each came up, this indicated ambiguity in the god's response—a kind of "yes and no" reply.

There were also several sets of divining sticks, or "fortune sticks," as they were sometimes called. Each set had several hundred sticks, and each stick was marked with a number in Chinese. The petitioner selected a set of sticks, shook the cup gently up and down in front of the shrine until one stick fell to the floor. He would then take that stick to Ing Hay, who would look up the corresponding number in one of several books containing a verse corresponding to each number. The verses were usually quite vague and cryptic and had to be interpreted by the priest.

Another method sometimes resorted to was to cast the *I-Ching*. The *I-Ching* is a very old book of wisdom, couched also in vague and poetical terms. Using a number of yarrow stalks, or wooden sticks, the priest slowly arrives at a series of numbers which eventually lead him to the book. The book might answer a question such as that actually asked, "Should I invest in a business in Baker, Oregon?" with a response like:

> There is a want of understanding between men. Its indication is unfavorable to the firm and correct course of the superior man. We see in it the great gone and the little come.

Again, with much discussion between the inquirer and the

priest, perhaps aided by the advice of bystanders, the answer would be interpreted in light of the question.

Ing Hay also had available more esoteric methods of fortune-telling. Many petitioners preferred a more direct way of communing with the gods, and for them, Ing Hay would set out on a table a number of printed sheets containing characters arranged at random in columns. He would then hold a long writing brush—or sometimes a wooden piece not unlike that used in the ouija board of western tradition—and the god's hand would guide his as the brush rose and fell, seemingly at random. Sometimes the message would be impossibly garbled; other times it would be clear and concise, giving obviously relevant responses. Hundreds of such sheets were found in the store, still bearing the original message from the Chinese gods.

To the western mind, with its more anthropomorphic and rational gods, the Chinese religions practiced in the Kam Wah Chung and its fortune-telling aspects seem mere superstition. We must remember, however, that there are aspects of our own religious practices which seem strange and incomprehensible to the outsider, and that Christian spiritualism is itself a very long and popular tradition. The Chinese who petitioned their god were also in a sense asking for the advice of the entire community, and in asking a question like "Should I invest in a business in Baker, Oregon?" the Chinese were also paying Ing Hay and Lung On a small sum for their own opinions. As they were two of the leaders of the Chinese community, their opinions were obviously valuable and in Lung On's case, with his great business acumen and wide circle of friends, probably very valuable indeed.

It is clear that the shrine in the Kam Wah Chung and Co. store served a number of very practical functions for the two men who ran it. As each petitioner paid about fifty cents for advice, it was a nice source of revenue. The entire community joined together in raising funds for the annual refurbishment of the shrine and for special festivals and ceremonies. The occasion also brought many people into the store who might not otherwise have come there. The constant questions asked of the god probably also gave Lung On and Ing Hay a real insight into the problems and state of affairs in the Chinese community, knowledge essential to their positions as community leaders. It is certain, however, that the main purpose of the shrine was religious and not political or economic. Long after most of the Chinese had died or returned home, Ing Hay, aged and blind, continued to worship before the shrine and to place daily the "Three Precious Things" before his god.

Perhaps the most important function of the building was its use as a social center. Chinese could come into the building, drink the tea recently imported from their homeland, consume an expensive delicacy, talk of the political situation back home, arrange loans or complicated business transactions, or if they were of a simpler turn of mind, drink and gamble.

Until American drug laws forbade it, the building was also a sort of opium den. Ing Hay and Lung On imported opium quite legally. The laborer could purchase a pipe of it, light up and "mount the dragon" in a drug-induced dream, and be temporarily wafted to his homeland. Whatever sounds filtered through to his ears would be the soft, lilting dialect of Toisan County and the smells would be those familiar from childhood: incense, soy, and cooking oils. If he occasionally opened his eyes, he would see a calendar from a Chinese bank, a moral maxim written in Lung On's strong hand, or other immigrants playing cards or sitting quietly beside the warmth of the stove.

4.
The Partners

After their arrival in 1887 and the purchase of Kam Wah Chung and Co., Ing Hay and Lung On must have felt that their future was very bright. The area had a relatively long history of productive gold mining, the Chinese community around them was numerous, and they were in a pivotal economic position in that community. Further booms would have led to more migration into the area, a larger clientele, and increased economic power and social status, but this was not to be. The gold booms were largely over, and the dominant factor for the rest of their lives was to be the constant shrinkage of the Chinese community of Eastern Oregon in general, and of John Day in particular. This shrinkage is made clear in the census figures. Following are the statistics for the total Chinese population in Oregon:

1860	425
1870	3,330
1880	9,510
1890	9,540
1900	10,397
1910	7,363
1920	3,090
1930	2,075

These figures, though, are undoubtedly highly inaccurate. Many Chinese had entered the country illegally and had become masters at avoiding official notice here. One problem in policing illegal aliens was the ease with which Chinese changed their names. It was customary for them to change their names at several important junctures in life, and considering the great many Chinese who bore the same surname, white agencies often became confused, as this article from the *Grant County News*, April 14, 1887, shows:

> Last Tuesday almost the entire day was consumed at the Court House by the attorneys endeavoring to find whether or not Git Lee was Ah Fong, or Ah Gi Git Lee, or Gi Lee Ah Bong, in the case of Clark vs. the Chinese companies.

Possibly there were about twice as many Chinese as were noted by the census takers. Statistics for the state as a whole show several patterns. Note that both Ing Hay and Lung On arrived after the great bulge of Chinese immigration into the state had passed. The critical years are those from 1870-80, after which time the Chinese population increased very slowly to 1900, then began to drop rapidly.

Let us now examine the statistics for Grant County, where John Day and Canyon City are located:

1870	946
1880	905
1890	326
1900	114
1910	37
1940	21*

* All non-whites together

Again, these figures are probably off by almost a factor of two, but we can assume that they are relatively accurate, or that about the same percentage of Chinese escaped the census taker's eye (and the immigration officer's) each census period. We know, for example, that there were at least 600 Chinese in Canyon City at the time of the fire in 1885, perhaps closer to 1,000, yet the census lists only 905 for the entire county in 1880, and only 326 in 1890. Nonetheless, the trend in Chinese population in Grant County was rapidly and irreversibly downward.

In comparing the statistics for Oregon and those for Grant

County, it is evident that while the total Chinese population in Oregon was increasing somewhat, it was decreasing rapidly in Grant County. Many of the Grant County Chinese were moving to the Portland area, whose Chinese population was increasing during the same period because of better opportunities for employment.

The reasons for Chinese fleeing Grant County were several. The most important was undoubtedly the scarcity of jobs. The pattern was for Chinese to take jobs as servants or semi-skilled laborers, and there were simply too few opportunities in Grant County. As transportation improved, it was no longer necessary for miners, loggers, and cowboys to spend long periods in remote camps. Also, the need for cooks, laundrymen, and the like decreased.

Another reason was social. There were very few Chinese women in Oregon. In 1910, of the total population of 7,363 Chinese, only 320 were female. More than seventy percent of the Chinese were single, compared to forty-four percent of the white population. In John Day, for example, despite the large size of the community in the nineteenth century, there seem never to have been more than a few women, and no baby was born of Chinese parents until after 1940.

A particular problem facing the Chinese was a traditional prohibition against marrying within the same name group. Thus, an Ing could not marry an Ing, even though their closest joint ancestor may have been dead for centuries. Because of family and village ties, Chinese tended initially to congregate with others from the same village or locality, which meant a high concentration of people with a relatively small number of names. What was an advantage at the outset soon became a real disadvantage as it greatly reduced the number of potential marriageable partners. The answer to both of these problems was, of course, to migrate to the urban areas.

The Chinese were not only constantly diminishing in absolute numbers but were also becoming an ever smaller proportion of the total population. While their presence and their culture had been important in the earlier period, as time went on they were simply overwhelmed and reduced to a colorful but largely unimportant minority group in the wider community.

As the opportunities for jobs shrank and as their relative importance and economic leverage in the area waned, the Chinese community fell on very hard times. Individuals who had left the Canton area as boys or young men, hopeful of making their fortunes and one day returning home wealthy, soon found that it was difficult to find even subsistence in America, the land of the "great gold mountain."

Many of these men were separated forever from their homeland by the poverty which kept them from ever returning. Their once bright hopes dashed, suicide came to be preferable to the dishonor of demeaning work or begging. Their depression grew worse in the period before their Lunar New Year, when all solid citizens were by tradition to pay their debts, buy new clothing, and make ritual visits to their friends. An example of such a suicide comes to us from the *Grant County News*, February 6, 1890:

> This is China New Year and they make quite a demonstration. A Chinaman, just before their holidays, was found dead. It is said that he had been unable to work and could not get money for the holidays and concluded to skip by taking poison.

There are many other cases of suicides from their period, and several incidents of men who went mad under the strain of living in such a difficult environment.

Like people everywhere who fall upon hard times, many Chinese were led into illegal activities in their efforts to survive. The Chinese community, of course, has a well-deserved reputation for being unusually law abiding. Its supportive institutions cushion economic troubles and give individual members the social involvement necessary for their physical and mental health. The Chinese community also had, especially in the nineteenth century, its share of hard cases. There were always, for example, plenty of toughs available to the tongs from which they could recruit their "highbinders," a term derived from their custom of tying up their queues before going into action. The community also had less fearsome toughs, or "boo hao doys," a term which might best be translated as "bad buys." These individuals had usually fled China because of involvement in crime or rebellion, and they soon turned to their old pursuits in this country. This violence and crime was most often restricted to the confines of the urban Chinatowns, but on the frontier, particularly in the declining economy of the 1880s and 1890s, there were occasional examples of it. In northern Idaho in the year 1887, when many of the mines were failing, so many Chinese began adulterating their gold dust by numerous stratagems that some people refused to take it in lieu of coin—as had always been the easy custom in the gold fields.

In 1886, a Chinese was arrested in Spokane Falls for changing a one-dollar note into a fifty by adding numerals taken from a government tax stamp. He passed the bill but was later apprehended. In September of 1890, a group of Chinese tunnelled into the First National Bank in The Dalles on the Columbia and escaped with almost ten thousand dollars in cash. Several were caught in Portland, with part of the money; others were apprehended in St. Paul, Minnesota, but released because of shaky evidence and the effort it would have taken to send them back to stand trial. One of the gang was eventually sentenced to two years in the state prison, but most of the money was never recovered.

The violent era of the gold camps and frontier towns did not pass without incident in the John Day Chinatown. There is an ill-documented but substantial story of a gambling fight in one of the smaller Chinese stores which adjoined Kam Wah Chung and Co. A local cowboy, or "buckaroo" as they were actually called, had a disagreement with an older Chinese man over the turn of a card. The buckaroo went for his gun but was stabbed in the throat before he could get the gun clear. The Chinese, hitherto regarded as a substantial member of the community,

fled and was never heard from again. The buckaroo lived and
so does the story.

Ing Hay and Lung On thus soon found themselves presiding
over an ever-smaller community. There were, occasionally,
hopeful signs. One such period of raised expectations came in
the 1890s. At that time there was another short mining boom in
the John Day area. Several mines where lode mining was pur-
sued hit rich veins.

In 1896, the Sumpter Valley Railroad arrived at Prairie City,
situated at the crest of the Blue Mountains, overlooking the
John Day area. The line was running south and was part of a
network of local narrow-gauge lines which it was hoped would
eventually tie into the Union Pacific and truly open up the
country. The railway was laid by a large contingent of the
familiar Chinese track men, and Lung On and Ing Hay must
have thought that many more Chinese would soon settle
amongst them. About 1900, the large lodes of the "Bonanza"
and the "North Pole" mines in Sumpter Valley began pro-
ducing. Ing Hay and Lung On were initially optimistic, as most
locals must have been, that the familiar cycle of boom and bust
was on the upswing for a change. So, they prepared for a new
influx of Chinese miners and laborers into the area.

As the two leading members of the Chinese community, Doc
Hay, its most accomplished professional, and Lung On, the
wealthy head of the Sze Yup District Association, they anticipated not only increased opportunities with a new wave of
immigration but added responsibilities. One of those responsibilities was to feed and house newcomers while helping
them find work. Thus, in the 1890s, the two men added a par-
tial second story to the Kam Wah Chung building. This was the
traditional pattern followed by local Chinese notables who
were expected to provide upstairs quarters for poor relatives
and itinerant newcomers.

The expected new migrants never arrived. The costs of
building the railroad were just too high, given the mountain
tunnels and steep grades required. It stopped in Prairie City,

and although it operated for some time, it never got any farther, and only a restored depot remains to mark the spot.
Neither did the mines attract the large numbers of Chinese that
the partners had anticipated; lode mining was capital intensive
and did not require large numbers of workers. In the declining
economy of the period, there was also much unemployment
among whites and consequently great resentment at firms
which hired Chinese. In any event, the small boom soon
faltered and by 1903 was in decline. The upstairs room became
a limited-use storeroom since it was an inconvenient place to
store bulky or heavy items, which had to be manhandled up the
narrow stairs. The room today looks almost as clean and unused
as in the year it was built in preparation for a new wave of
Chinese who never came.

The John Day Chinatown, which had been in 1887 a thriving, independent community, began to shrink rapidly. The
population dropped from the approximately five to six hundred of 1885 to less than one hundred by 1900. A travelling
historian wrote in the *Illustrated History* of the community on
his visit in 1900:

> At present there are perhaps a hundred Chinamen in John
> Day. They have their own stores, three in number, and the com-
> munity is apart from the main town. The inhabitants of this
> quaint settlement are orderly and apparently contented, and
> while, as is their way, they do not mingle with Americans nor
> do they adopt American manners and customs, they are not
> considered a detriment to the town.

As the Chinese community shrank, the surrounding white
community expanded. The Chinese fish and duck ponds—actually old pits left behind by gold dredges—fell into disuse and
were eventually filled in. The small shacks which had been the
homes of Chinese bachelors fell empty and were either torn
down for the lumber, burned, or converted into storage sheds
and garages by whites.

There had been a small communal temple outside, within about thirty feet of the Kam Wah Chung and Co. Building, but soon there were not enough adherents to support it, and it too fell into disuse. The practice of religion became centered completely on the small altar in the Kam Wah Chung Building. As several fires broke out over the years, the community became even smaller. By 1940, it was reduced to fewer than twenty men, most quite advanced in age and living in either the Kam Wah Chung or in rented quarters in the town proper. Today the city park of John Day stands where the early Chinese community once flourished.

Traditional Chinese ancestor worship and the social practices of village China demanded that the bones of all family members eventually be returned to the plots where generations of family members were interred. As the Chinese of John Day died, some were first buried in the local area. Others were cremated over a slow fire which left the bones intact; then the bones were returned to China for final burial. Finally, virtually all of the bones of those initially buried in John Day were disinterred and shipped home through funeral parlors in Portland which were accustomed to the Chinese funeral practices.

The disintegration of John Day was not much different from the death of many of the smaller mining towns dotted about the Blue Mountains. Austin, Bonanza, Bourne, Granite, Greenhorn, Raw Dog, Yellow Dog, and Marysville were once as alive and populous as the John Day Chinatown and, today, are even deader.

From one perspective, the decline in the Chinese population of Eastern Oregon was a disaster for those who remained; their culture and their community was approaching a point where it could no longer be sustained. From another point of view, however, there was an advantage. While the whites had been worried that they themselves might be overwhelmed by masses of Oriental immigrants in the 1860s and 1870s, by the end of the 1880s it was obvious that there was no such danger; that it was the Chinese who were failing. In 1888, the immigration laws were further tightened, and the series of laws enacted during the 1880s, the Exclusion Acts, began to take effect. Chinese immigration dropped to a trickle. With the decline of mining, far more Chinese began to leave eastern Oregon than came in. The white community began to be less fearful, and with less fear came more empathy and understanding. The whites began to see the Chinese as the asset which they had always been to the region.

In the earlier period there are isolated examples of statements favoring the Chinese or, at least, some of their qualities. The widespread violence sometimes directed at Chinese in the cities during the early 1880s never attracted favorable comment on the frontier. There, law and order, peace and stability were conspicuous by their absence and many people paradoxically valued them far more than did those who lived in more settled areas. The whites of the frontier usually argued in their newspapers that law had to be upheld, even if it sometimes benefited the often unwelcome Chinese immigrant. Whites also recognized that much of the agitation against the Chinese was spurious, as shown in this article from the *Grant County News*, August 12, 1886:

> The class of men who made the row about the Chinese last winter won't work now that they have a chance. But in the winter, when they can no longer sleep in the open air, or pick up a living anywhere, they will organize again into "workingmen's associations," and begin to howl about the Chinese.

As the 1880s wore on, whites became more and more inclined to be positive about the Chinese in their midst. One begains to see articles which, although referring in a generally negative way to the Chinese, nonetheless mention their "go-ahead" qualities. When the immigration laws were tightened and enforced, some people began to see the remaining Chinese an endangered asset, as can be seen in this article from the *Grant County News* of December 27, 1888:

Shooting cattle, horses, Chinamen and sheep on the range and dogging stock off government land seems to be the manner in which some Longcreek braves spend their leisure hours. Stockmen say that since the Chinese Exclusion bill became a law, Chinamen are scarce and, therefore, warn all parties not to kill Mongolians in their employ, or they will be prosecuted to the full extent of the law.

From the year 1890 on, newspapers give the impression that for the first time Chinese were being accorded full protection of the law in Eastern Oregon. Cases began to occur in which whites were arrested and jailed for beating up Chinese. Compare, for example, these two examples. The first is taken from the *Grant County News* for July 31, 1884:

A man by the name of Vickers became a little "how-came-you-so" out at Burns last Sunday and came near "taking the town." A Chinaman was considerably battered.

This one is from the same paper, November 6, 1890:

Joe Masterson was tried before Judge Rulison last week for an unprovoked assault on a Chinaman, and fined $25.00 and costs.

Although whites were growing more tolerant of the Chinese in their midst, occasional acts showed that many still did not accept the Chinese as fully human. Letters at the Oregon Historical Society tell part of this story and interviews with members of the white community fill in the remainder. Sometime between 1894 and 1905, a Chinese named Kung-lin was shot and killed. The Chinese community was very resentful and thought of the act as murder, as shown in several letters exchanged between John Day and friends and relatives of the deceased in China, but an interview conducted in 1976 gave a slightly different view. Our informant had, as a younger person, talked to the man who had done the shooting. The man had seen the Chinese fishing in one of the old dredge ponds and fired a high-caliber rifle into the water, intending to frighten him. The bullet ricocheted and killed the Chinese instantly. The white man told the story without guilt and with some amusement before his own death in the 1940s.

The decline of the Chinese community and the mining industry on which its members depended had different effects on the survivors. While Chinatown grew smaller and economically less powerful as the need for its labor declined, the white community grew larger and more orderly. While the Chinese community of the 1880s had been exotic and colorful, it was no more so than the often violent bars of adjoining white communities like Canyon City. As the frontier passed, however, and families and churches came in, the demand for law and order and social conformity grew.

A common source of trouble between the two groups was the Chinese use of opium. Many of the Chinese who came to this country brought both their addiction and the drug with them. One of the first notices taken of opium in the John Day region occurs in 1885, at the Lunar New Year festival. A reporter for the *Grant County News* wrote up his experience there on February 19, 1885:

> Last Friday the Chinamen commenced the celebration of a feast commonly known as the Chinese New Year. A News reporter visited their habitations last Sunday afternoon and found the Celestials in the midst of their festivities. On every hand there were to be found dishes of rice, plates of nameitandtakeit, and burning tapers, while the moon-eyed denizens of the town were stretched on beds and bunks, indulging in tobacco, opium, whiskey and other narcotics. At this season the usual parsimonious Chinaman is always liberal to a certain degree, and our reporter was offered several cigars, quite a quantity of candy, several cupfuls of "China gin," and was even offered the privilege of a pull at their opium pipes. The devotees of the pipe were all busily engaged in their favorite pastime and several of them seemed to be under the influence of the drug.
>
> To prove what a curse the Chinaman is in introducing the life

and soul-destroying habit of opium smoking, we have only to cite one instance that came under our notice.

We were accompanied by a nine-year-old boy to whom the pipe was freely offered, and indeed, he was frequently importuned to partake of its intoxication. If they are so liberal in bestowing their favors upon boys, would they not be so with youths of a more susceptible and inquisitive age, and thus sow the seeds of a life of dissipation and disgrace?

It is noteworthy that however outraged the reporter was in 1885, at that time opium smoking was still legal, and the Chinese could indulge themselves as they wished. For them it was a social ritual which linked them not only to each other but to their homeland, and it was a means of escape from the harsh realities of the frontier life they lived. It is also true that opium smoking is not as addictive as we sometimes believe; true addiction had to wait for the widespread use of the hypodermic needle.

The whites, of course, found their own addiction to alcohol to be socially acceptable and even somewhat comical. As the frontier filled up, however, the opium use of the Chinese began to seem less harmless. Laws were passed to forbid its unlicensed importation in the mid-1880s, and prosecutions began in 1886 in Grant County. A nation-wide reform movement began to concentrate upon opium abuse in the late nineteenth century, and state laws were passed well in advance of the Federal Pure Food and Drug Act of 1906, which made opium illegal. It should be noted that there was a clear element of hypocrisy in focusing upon the Chinese. More than one informant in the area mentioned that some whites used opium in its pure form, so we must assume that many more used the various patent medicines of the period which were opium based.

In April of 1905, a mob gathered and broke into the Kam Wah Chung and Co. building. Several Chinese, including Lung On—who, ironically did not use the drug—were hauled off to jail. The excited mob initially ordered the entire Chinese community to get out of town, a town which they had esentially founded, it should be noted. Lung On quickly got competent legal assistance from a local law firm. The lawyers raised a blizzard of objections, even trying to generate pressure from the Chinese Embassy in Washington, and succeeded in getting the case dismissed. The Chinese offered the community a face-saving contribution to the local education fund and the matter was forgotten.

Ing Hay was told by the State of Oregon that opium was now a controlled substance and that a register of sales had to be kept. Witnesses differ as to whether or not Ing Hay stopped smoking opium at this point. We know from other incidents that he had tremendous self-control and doubtless could have stopped had he wished to do so. Some family members insist that he stopped immediately; other witnesses state that he continued to use it for some time. Certainly we know that other members of the Chinese community did continue to smoke it, although very circumspectly.

During this period of the turn of the century, as the Chinese community in John Day began to decline, its surviving members began to seem more human to the surrounding white community. It is from this time that individual members of the little Chinatown began to take on a real identity and to emerge from the faceless laboring masses of the gold fields. Although we can really know only Ing Hay and Lung On with sufficient certainty to write a biography, several other members of the community are worthy of mention. These individuals were all remarkable people in their own right, each a pioneer of the early days of the frontier. Under slightly different circumstances we might have had enough information to give them a much more substantial treatment. Here we can only list them with a few pertinent facts and stories which were told about them to our interviewers. The important fact about them all is that none of them was a stereotypical "Chinaman," and each is warmly remembered by at least several members of the surviving community of John Day and Canyon City.

Buckaroo Sam was one of several Chinese who worked as cowhands on ranches in the area around John Day. He worked on the Stewart ranch for several years but also on other ranches and farms in the area. He was a small man who loved to ride and seems to have earned his name Buckaroo. Early in his career as a cowhand, Buckaroo Sam was bucked off a horse and cut badly on his face. The scar drew his face down on one side so that he appeared to talk out of the side of his mouth. People who knew him said that he was very homely and difficult to understand.

Later, when Buckaroo Sam was herding sheep for another rancher, he had a second accident in which he lost his thumbs. He was riding a horse behind the herd of sheep and was holding onto the saddlehorn. He got a loop of rope around his thumbs and when his horse jumped unexpectedly over a log, both thumbs were jerked off.

Old-timers recall that for some reason Buckaroo Sam did not live in Chinatown. Some say that he was an outcast because he was a buckaroo, but others say they do not know because the Chinese kept their arguments to themselves. Sam did, however, stay with a white family in John Day in his later years, either by choice or because he was an outcast from the Chinese community.

Then there was Big Sam and he was what his name implies —big. He was supposedly well over six feet. He had a queue when he first arrived in John Day but gradually cut it until it was gone. It is said that he was not as friendly as the other residents of Chinatown. He kept to himself more, had a garden, and sometimes did the cooking for Doc Hay in the early days. Eye witnesses claim that the other Chinese did not seem to care much for him. This may have been because of his lower social status as a servant to the Chinese themselves.

A description of a Chinese funeral given to one of our interviewers could be about Big Sam's funeral:

Well, I can tell you about a Chinese funeral that was kinda

funny. The man who run the hardware store then was the undertaker. We didn't have it like it is now—just made the wood-
en boxes; and this old Chinaman—he was rather tall—so I guess
they got the box a little short for him—I was standing there
watching them. There was three or four Chinamen standing
around there. They laid him in, got his head down, and then his
knees kinda stuck up a little so she [sic] just reached over and
pushed his knees down—and then his head popped up!! Those
Chinamen, they just kiyied, and they didn't know what to think.
It was just done so suddenlike—pushed the knees down, something had to give . . . .

In the early years of the Chinese community, 1862-93, there
was a Chinese who was believed to be married. Mr. Bong Gee
was not only a successful businessman but supposedly had two
wives. In 1886, the local papers found this to be most interesting and rejoiced in the good copy occasioned by the elopement
of Gee's second wife. In the *Grant County News*, Canyon
City, Thursday, September 2, 1886, it was noted:

Bong Gee of this city recently sent $500 below to purchase
himself a new wife. Mrs. Bong Gee number 2 arrived in due
time, but after meeting her liege lord she was not content with
her surroundings. She ran away with a handsomer man whereat
Mr. Bong Gee mourns.

This account is at once humorous and condescending in tone.
However, it does assume that people of Grant County in 1886
knew Bong Gee and would be interested, if not a little titillated,
by this piece of marital trouble, Chinese style.

Three years later, Bong Gee, so-called marital problems once
again made the news. The following is from the *Grant County
News*, Canyon City, Thursday, August 15, 1889:

Chinese residents of John Day were considerably worked up
the latter part of last week over an elopement in high life. One
of Bong Gee's wives ran away with He Hong. Bong Gee cared

not so much for the severing of affection as for the severing of his finance, and kicked up a row about it and threatened to murder Mrs. Gee and Mr. Hong, for she was possessed of great wealth, the proceeds of several gambling dens, which wealth her spouse desired to retain in the Bong Gee family.

All was settled without the shedding of blood, however, and upon the promise of Mr. Gee that he would not harm a hair of her que [sic], neither one of He Hong's, his erring partner returned to her place in the domestic circle of Bong Gee, and lived happily ever after.

The article shows little if no sympathy or understanding of Chinese customs. The article mentions that Mrs. Bong Gee was wealthy from proceeds from gambling dens and that Bong Gee's disturbance was worry over loss of his wife's fortune. Wives in China at that time had no property rights whatsoever. Bong Gee's wife's alleged fortune belonged to Bong Gee outright by Chinese custom, law, and practice. In certain unusual circumstances the dowry which a woman brought with her when she married would be returned to her and to her family, but this happened rarely. The news article quoted has an almost sneering tone, as though the reporter were laughing up his sleeve at the troubles Bong Gee kept having with his wives. No sensitivity is shown either for Bong Gee's loss of face among the Chinese and in the white community, or for the woman who may well have had reason to seek another male's company and protection.

Perhaps it was Bong Gee who was laughing up his sleeve at the news reporter and his interpretation of what had occurred. The 1880 United States census of Grant County listed eight Chinese women in Grant County, approximately one half of whom gave prostitute, whore, courtesan, or worker in a bawdy house as occupation. None of the women was listed as wife. Ignoring the gross ignorance and blatant prejudice of the census takers, one would have to accept these figures as at least partly reflecting the communities canvassed. It could be equally true that Bong Gee's success in business was partly due to having prostitutes for hire. Bong Gee's so-called second wife most likely was a second prostitute brought in to add new blood to his already thriving business. She also could have been hired to help the first woman or even to work for her. Bong Gee's first "wife" allegedly had great wealth from the proceeds of several gambling dens, which could also have provided female services to the many miners of the Chinese community.

The early Chinese community in the John Day area consisted mainly of male miners (1870—99%; 1880—98.3%) drawn by the lure of fortunes made in gold. Too, the females who came into the United States at first were rarely respectable, traditional wives. Most wives remained in China to care for parents, children, what property the couple might have had, and to conduct the ancestor rites. The males ventured out to the "Land of the Gold Mountain" to seek their fortunes, most often intending to return home to China, as the majority eventually did. These men would expect to have some female companions during their stay in America.

In China, prostitution was a recognized profession. People in traditional China did not marry for romantic reasons but for economic and family ones. It was assumed that if a man wanted to pursue romantic or sexual interests, he would do so. Second marriages were common for this reason, and many times the male chose for his second wife a favorite singing girl or prostitute. Thus, for the prostitute, there was the possibility of, if not the hope for, a marriage and security.

It would seem then that Bong Gee's wives could very possibly have been former prostitutes at the least, and more likely were practicing prostitutes and not his wives at all. Bong Gee, being knowledgeable about the white community and its prejudices, would then have referred to the women as "wives" rather than explaining their true relationship. According to Stanford Lyman, an expert on Asians in America, many of the Chinese women brought to the United States were under contract as servants and were put to work in brothels. This would better explain Bong Gee's worry in both incidents as due to the loss of income and not alienation of affection or embarrassment.

What the news reporters of these two incidents saw as a peculiar Chinese lack of affection would be better understood as irritation over loss of income and investment. Perhaps, in both cases, the other men had become enamored with these women, maybe the only females in the Chinese community, and had approached Bong Gee, offering to buy their contracts. Bong Gee, being a good businessman and hating to lose a steady income, would have refused. Then, in desperation, the women and their lovers could have fled, hoping to find a new life elsewhere; or the lover, wanting her for himself, could have kidnapped the woman. Bong Gee, having the influence that money brings, could then have enlisted the aid of other Chinese males who perhaps did not want to be deprived of the women's attentions, and the fleeing lovers would have been apprehended. There would be no chance for a new life in the new land.

The uproar noted by the reporter of the second event is easily explained. The loss of the available women, either as wives or prostitutes, would have disrupted the social scene in John Day's Chinatown. Rival claims for control over prostitutes or a woman were common causes of violence in America's Chinatowns.

Then there was Charlie Po Kee, the Chinese laundryman of John Day. He, like Big Sam, is supposed to be one of the group of Chinese who came to John Day from Astoria. Charlie also is said to have dealt in a small way in the bootleg whiskey business. However, Charlie Po Kee's greatest claim to fame is that he had a wife who helped him in the laundry.

Though eight Chinese women were noted in the 1880 census in Grant County, none were listed as married. The only married Chinese woman in the area appeared in the 1880 records for Baker County, where eight of a total of thirty-one Chinese females were married. The only Chinese woman remembered from John Day's Chinatown was Crazy Jane, wife of the laundryman, Charlie Po Kee. According to eyewitness reports, Crazy Jane got her name because she would run when anyone approached her and was rarely ever seen out alone. Other accounts say that she was not friendly, that she would not speak and would not look a person in the eye.

Not understanding traditional Chinese customs regarding married women, the townspeople of John Day called a Chinese woman who behaved in such bizarre fashion "crazy." But Crazy Jane was, in fact, behaving according to Chinese custom. A married woman in traditional China was not permitted out of her courtyard. If the woman had to go out, to be considered respectable she had to veil her face heavily and ride in a sedan chair, not walk. Naturally, it would be most unseemly to speak to strangers under any conditions. It is most likely that Crazy Jane—being the sole example of a respectable married woman in Chinatown—would be, according to Chinese custom, very circumspect in her behavior.

In *Daughter of Han*, one of the most detailed works about the daily life of Chinese women, the narrator tells of a crazy woman in her town. This woman went out one day for a walk beyond her courtyard and to the market without covering her face. The townspeople set up a cry for all to come see the crazy woman. Apparently "crazy" can be applied in different ways by different cultures. Crazy Jane probably never knew that her respectable deportment earned her the label of a crazy woman. Although her peculiarities were harmless, the name took on a life of its own. Thus, people who did not know Crazy Jane well would assert that indeed she was crazy.

A person who lived in the Chinatown district in John Day during her youth recalls that Crazy Jane, like most of the Chinese, was friendly to children. She remembers that, on occasion, Crazy Jane would give tangerines or candy to children venturing into Chinatown. She also recalls that Crazy Jane dressed "like some American women do now—slacks or pants pretty loose and a jacket. She wore that kind of outfit all the time." However, she says that Crazy Jane seemed to favor the boys over the girls and attributes that to the fact that boys were better liked by the Chinese.

The decline of the John Day Chinatown after 1887 might have meant the decline of Ing Hay and Lung On. Certainly the Kam Wah Chung and Co. business was hard hit by the rapid erosion of its economic base as its Chinese customers died, returned to China, or moved to Portland. Lesser men might have sold out and moved on, but Ing Hay and Lung On were not lesser men. They began to shift their economic base and their way of life so as not only to survive but to improve their lot in John Day. Lung On, adaptable and intelligent, was to become a major businessman, including among his many interests the first automobile dealership in Eastern Oregon. Ing Hay was to become increasingly well known as "Doc Hay," the China doctor, the most respected medical man for hundreds of miles around.

5.
Herbalist and Pulsologist

Ing Hay's fame and success as an herbal doctor have fostered many legends about how he actually became a traditional Chinese herbalist. Hay himself, in later years, contributed to the romantic stories about his beginnings. One such story, told by Hay, claims that he came from a long line of famous herbalists in China. Another story claims that he returned to China to study and perfect his skills as an herbal doctor, later returning to John Day to continue his practice. A third account says that he learned herbal medicine and pulse diagnosis in John Day from an older Chinese named Doc Lee. Doc Lee is supposed to have given his own book of medicinal herbs and prescriptions—which is still in the Kam Wah Chung Building today—to Ing Hay.

Doc Hay did indeed come from a family of herbalists. Two of his nephews followed in his footsteps here in the United States, one even taking over his practice in John Day in later years. Since Hay's family came from a district in China which is known for herbalists, Hay would have had some exposure and training before he decided to seek his fortune in the gold fields of Eastern Oregon. When he arrived there, he did at first do common labor, but he soon had the good fortune to meet Doc Lee, who was already a famous doctor among the Chinese in the gold fields.

Hay's nephew claims that it was under Lee's instruction that Hay perfected his craft. However, though one can learn herbal medicine from another person, only a very few people are born with the gift for pulse diagnosis, or "pulsology" as it is sometimes called. Ing Hay was one of the gifted few born to be a pulse-diagnosis practitioner. His heightened sense of touch gave him an innate skill that, under the guidance of a master such as Doc Lee, needed only demonstration and correction to be perfected. Hay's former patients remember his touch to be the softest in their experience. Doc Lee must have delighted in his young apprentice's gift for the time-honored art of pulse diagnosis—discovered in a poor miner's calloused hands leagues away from their homeland.

Traditional Chinese herbal medicine is not a folk medicine like that in the West. It is a well-organized body of medical knowledge based on observations, experiments, and clinical trials. These have been recorded, and medical theories have evolved from conclusions based on the observations and tests.

The *Nei Ching*, written two thousand years ago, is an eighteen-volume compilation of all Chinese medical knowledge up to that time. It is a comprehensive work on anatomy and physiology. However, it is more concerned with general principles of health and the human body than with specific therapeutics. The principle of harmony within the body's processes is stressed in this study, which regards disruption of the body's harmony as the cause of disease. This is the central theory of all later Chinese medicine. Pulse diagnosis, the chief method of diagnosis used in the *Nei Ching*, is the keystone of Chinese traditional medicine. The doctor skilled in pulse diagnosis can, without ever speaking to the patient and simply by touching the radial artery of the wrist, arrive at a correct diagnosis in minutes.

Some old-timers claim Hay said that in China a student doctor had three chances to pass his examinations on pulse diagnosis. The patient stuck his hand through a hole in a curtain blocking him from sight, and the student doctor was supposed to diagnose the patient's illness just from his pulse. Pulse diagnosis was both a science and an art. It was so sensitive a method of diagnosis that, according to Dr. Felix Mann, a noted British physician who has made a study of traditional Chinese medicine, pulse diagnosis could detect past ailments. Thus, a doctor could recount his patient's past medical history and could warn of future illnesses.

Former patients of Doc Hay state that he often told them what was wrong with them before they said anything to him. In fact, Hay delighted in surprising his patients with this diagnostic technique. He would refuse to let his patients tell him what was wrong but would insist upon telling them what their symptoms were.

There are four principal pulse types. *Fu* is a superficial, light, flowing pulse, described in *The Yellow Emporer's Classic of Internal Medicine* as being "like wood floating on water." *Ch'en* is a deeply impressed pulse "like a stone thrown into water." *Ch'ih,* the third pulse, is slow, with three beats to one cycle of respiration. The last, *Shu,* is a quick pulse with six beats to one breathing cycle. Pulsology charts three pulse points along the radial artery of each wrist, which indicate the functions of different organs in the body. These three spots on each wrist have a deep and a superficial reading, making a total of twelve different pulses. These can be divided further into twenty-eight qualities of pulse.

Traditional Chinese medicine viewed the pulse diagnosis as the essential information device through which to gain the patient's medical history—past, present and future. Doc Hay was a master of this technique. He would try to forecast the probable course and termination of the disease, making a prognosis in the tradition of Chinese medical practices. To accomplish this, the traditional Chinese doctor examined the patient by inspecting all the orifices and limbs (wang); hearing and smelling the patient's voice and breath (wen); and noting the palpation of the thorax and abdomen (tsie). Often "wen" was omitted, since pulsology or sphygmology (the scientific study of the pulse) provided a diagnosis of the ailment without relying on the patient himself.

Though born with the gift of pulse diagnosis, Hay did not leave his talent to the direction of the Fates. He took special care of his hands. Wing Wah, his nephew, recalls that Hay would never handle anything that was rough in nature, including coarse paper, which will rub the sensitive skin from one's fingertips. The nephew said, "Oh, now he would wear a glove on his hand; just keep his hand in good shape, just like a movie star or a woman, never handled anything rough."

To be able to function in the Wild West without handling anything rough would have been difficult for Doc Hay had it not been for his good friend and partner, Lung On. Lung On was indispensable to Hay's medical practice, not only for his handling of the rough work involved in the selection and preparation of the herbal prescriptions under Doc Hay's careful scrutiny, but in other ways as well. One witness said that Lung On even acted as a druggist's helper, packing the medicines around for Hay to protect those precious hands for the sensitive art of pulse diagnosis. Doc Hay also depended on Lung On to drive him about, first by horse and buggy, then in an automobile. When seriously ill patients sent for the China doctor, he arrived only because Lung On saw to it.

Lung On also handled the business correspondence in both Chinese and English. Doc Hay, of course, had primary contact with the patients, but his English was never very good. "Please send me directions how to use that medicine Hay gave me as I did not understand him," wrote Mr. D. C. Martin on October 22, 1905. Other letters seeking clarification from Lung On about Hay's instructions were also found in the Kam Wah Chung Building. Most letters from Hay's patients were addressed to both men, acknowledging Lung On as a crucial link in the transactions between the China doctor and his patients.

Chinese herbal pharmacology is a complex and highly developed science. The earliest pharmacopeia, or book on drugs, is *Pen-ts'ao ching*, attributed to Shen-nung, who probably wrote it in the first century B.C. It classifies 365 drugs into "superior" or nontoxic herbs, "medium" or relatively nontoxic herbs, and "inferior" or poisonous herbs—to be used to treat only very serious illnesses. The so-called "inferior" herbs produce a harsh effect upon the body, which is contrary to the traditional Chinese medical principle of maintenance of physical balance and harmony.

By the sixteenth century, *General Principles of Pharmacology (Pen-ts'ao kang-mu* had been written, which listed 1,892 substances. Most of these herbs were of vegetable origin from which 8,160 prescriptions were concocted. This pharmacopeia took Li Shin-chen twenty-six years to write and research. To date, Chinese herbalists and doctors have succeeded in collecting and classifying over two thousand different herbs that are traditionally used. The collection of herbs and other medications left by Doc Hay in the Kam Wah Chung and Co. Building totaled over five hundred. This represents what is probably the most extensive collection of traditional Chinese herbs in the Western Hemisphere.

Several herbs found in the Kam Wah Chung and Co. Building which were fairly easy to identify by name and medicinal use were marijuana or "yellow hemp" rhubarb or "yellow" efficacy," strychnine or "bitter-seeded Persian bean," and ginseng. The medicinal uses of marijuana in the treatment of glaucoma are being tested now by the United States Government. It has also long been used for its tranquilizing effects—doubtless the use to which Doc Hay put it in his complex herbal preparations.

Rhubarb or "yellow efficacy" was not used so much for its purgative properties as for its tonic powers upon the digestive tract. Hay included it in prescriptions for women's diseases, especially those resulting in the congestion of the pelvic organs. Fully one third of Hay's patients were women suffering from what people would call "women's complaints," complications resulting from childbirth or menstrual problems.

The kernels of the poisonous seeds of the plant *strychnos nux-vomica* (strychnine) were considered useful by the traditional Chinese doctor in the treatment of 120 diseases, especially throat infections. The kernels were ground into a fine powder and then blown into the throat. A former patient described the treatment Doc Hay gave for sore throats:

> . . . then he had some kind of red powder he blew in their throat. And it worked. It would stop it. He had a quill, and then

he sold these quills with [it] . . . . if you run across any of this red powder in little strips of paper, wrapped up, that's what it was for.

The powder from these kernels was also put into a composition of ointments to lessen swellings.

Ginseng was once reserved for the treatment of the emperor and members of the imperial family. It was the medicine to use when all other drugs failed. Ginseng is supposed to have stimulant, tonic, and restorative properties. Chinese herbalists would prescribe it for nearly every kind of disease of a severe nature. However, ginseng could only be administered at certain stages of a disease, the proper stage varying with each illness. At present, ginseng is used to treat hypertension and is prescribed as a tonic in cardiac conditions.

The traditional Chinese herbal doctor based his medical prognosis or predictions on the therapeutic principle, *Fu Chen P'ei Ben.* When a person is ill, so the principle goes, his body functions are abnormal and his vitality and resistance are low. The doctor's duty is to return the patient's body to normal and to increase his vitality and resistance. As one of Doc Hay's patients said, "What he really done was worked on your blood, to clear your blood up. Sometimes it took quite a while, but he sure was good at it."

The basic principle of Chinese herbal medicine is that the medication must constantly be adapted to each patient's condition and illness, and also to the course of the disease and each phase in its development. The complex herbal prescriptions, which were composed of many ingredients, reinforced beneficial action and neutralized unfavorable side effects within the body; the maintenance of harmony was always of the utmost importance in Chinese herbal practice. Some of Doc Hay's prescriptions had as many as eighty ingredients in them. One prescription he made in 1906 for a patient suffering from swollen feet contained eighty-three different herbs.

Though there are pills and powders in Chinese pharmacology, the characteristic method of dispensing medication is in a boiled broth made from the ingredients. However, Doc Hay is remembered for the powder he prescribed for sore throats and for a dried-prune-like lozenge he instructed his patients to suck. They claim it tasted as though alum were in it. Most often, though, Hay prescribed herbs that were to be boiled into a broth. It is remembered that, at first, he would cook up the medicine right in the Kam Wah Chung and Co. Building. This required patients to remain in John Day so they could go down to Chinatown for their daily doses of medicine. In later years, he would prepare the prescriptions in packages and the patient himself would boil up the brew at home. A former patient was once asked if he knew what Doc Hay had given him for treatment. He replied:

> No, we never did know—just herbs that was in there—he'd mix it up and give it to me. They cooked the medicine there at that time . . . . Doc Hay would fix it all up and he done the cooking. And then they'd put it in quart beer bottles, and that's the way they delivered it around town. There was about three doses in one of those quarts. You poured it out in a cup and warmed it up before you drank it.

Doc Hay is almost a prototype of the legendary country doctor who just happened to be a Chinese herbalist and pulsologist. People in the John Day area revere his memory and regale the visitor with tales of the cures he administered. His practice, if mapped, would extend from the Walla Walla, Washington, area in the north to the Nevada border in the south, and from Portland in the west to Payette, Idaho, in the east. He also treated people in Seattle, Astoria, and Klamath Falls. There is a record of a doctor from San Francisco consulting Doc Hay in 1903 about the treatment for sore throats. He even prepared a corn treatment for someone as far away as Terry, South Dakota!

Though Hay's medical practice covered a large territory, the convenient location of the Kam Wah Chung and Co. Building on the major shipping routes made it easy for isolated people to contact Doc Hay when in need of medical attention. Rather than ride for several days to the doctor, which in many cases would have killed them, Doc Hay's patients could write to him and describe their illness, then have him diagnose their disease and mail them medicine. Hay appears to have mastered the two difficulties of country practice: transportation and the cure.

In December of 1901, a Mr. Miller of Burns, Oregon, wrote to Lung On and Doc Hay to let them know that his sick wife and he had arrived safely in Burns after a two-day wagon trip from John Day. He mentions, though, that his wife was extremely tired from the journey but was taking her medicine carefully. One cannot help wondering what a two-day wagon journey in December from John Day to Burns would do to the recuperative powers of a seriously ill person.

In the early days of his medical practice, Doc Hay made house calls to distant places or to the seriously ill. One letter to Lung On asks that Hay and he "come over just as soon as you get this letter." This was written by Amy Williams of Beech Creek, Oregon, in late November 1904. Beech Creek is thirty miles from John Day. In late November, given the winter weather and the primitive roads, the trip would have been an ordeal for a healthy person, let alone someone who was ill. Seven miles per hour was good time for a team in cold weather on good roads; on muddy or snow-covered roads, the average was two and one-half miles per hour. To trust that one letter would bring the doctor speaks for the care and concern people *knew* Hay would extend them.

In a letter dated July 14, 1904, another patient argues for a reduced fee for her medicine since Hay would not have to come out to see her. With his record, Hay most likely was persuaded by her argument. During the winter months people would write to Hay for medicine to be sent by mail or the stage from as near by as Canyon City. A Mrs. Sollinger of Canyon City even specified that Hay send her medicine by Tom Morrison, the Burns driver on the stage.

Besides being on the transportation routes, Doc Hay's mail-order medical practice was additionally attractive to people because of his ability to diagnose illness from just one visit and a pulse reading, and even from cursory descriptions of the ailment in letters. One such letter reads in entirety: "Ma's tongue is coated so bad it is right white." As there was a date and postmark on this letter, one can assume Hay knew to whom to respond, but any diagnosis based on that description would have to be the product of genius and great intuition.

Since Hay practiced traditional Chinese herbal medicine, he was able to prescribe preparations that would work beneficially on weak constitutions and counteract negative reactions without endangering his patients' lives. He instructed his patients to give their reactions to his herbal prescriptions, which they did in their letters to him. Thus, there is ample evidence that Hay kept track of his mail-order patients by mail, to follow the course of their diseases and their reactions to the cures he prescribed.

Another important factor in the success and fine reputation of Doc Hay's medical business was the state of medical practice in the United States at the turn of the century. American medicine as such did not exist until the twentieth century. The primary responsibility for rendering medical care in the late 1800s and early 1900s was in the hands of domestic or part-time medical practitioners. The medical expert, Dr. Arthur Hertzler, commented that nineteenth century medicine was often a matter of luck, and the cure hardly distinguishable from the disease. Although medicine advanced greatly as a science in the nineteenth century, patients did not benefit from those advances until thirty years into the twentieth century. The development of the theory of bacterial cause of infectious disease and antibiotics; the refinement of the art of surgery through antisepsis or sterilization of hands, tools, and environment, and the use of anesthetics are seen as some of the most influential changes in medicine during that time period.

Most doctors of that period had not attended medical school.

They had read or studied medicine with some active doctor—but many just bought a book! Rapid western expansion and the resulting lack of legal regulations lowered educational standards in the medical schools across the country. Between 1800 and 1900, four hundred of them had been established in the United States. But the public developed a distrust in the skills of medical doctors, and many preferred help from other kinds of healers and physicians. Doc Hay was one of those sought for treatment of disease during this rise in competition between sectarian healers and medical school doctors.

Hay used the ancient pulse diagnosis technique as was previously stated. Such diagnosis can provide the patient's medical history as well as tell the master practitioner what is wrong and right with the patient. Chinese medicine stresses that a superior physician prevents illness by controlling it in its latent state and by seeing signs of it before it appears. By this definition, Hay was a superior physician. One of his former patients said that if you went to a white doctor, the first thing he would ask was where do you hurt, but Hay would just feel your pulse and then could tell you right where you hurt. Another patient described Hay's pulse technique this way: "Dr. Hay could feel your pulse and tell you what was wrong with you and that is no lie. He could tell if a woman was pregnant and the sex of the child."

A judge in Grant County also corroborates the claim that Doc Hay could foretell the sex of the fetus because he did it for him when his wife was pregnant with one of their children. A patent medicine advertisement of the 1940s, found in the Kam Wah Chung and Co. Building, told about Ing Hay's fine herbal practice and his ability to diagnose by pulse. It stated how Hay diagnosed a World War I veteran's stiff neck by saying that it was caused by shell shrapnel embedded in the veteran's neck. This diagnosis was later corroborated by X-rays taken at a hospital. The advertisement also stated that, in another pulse diagnosis, Hay told a woman, mother of four, that she had had five children. At first she said no, but Hay insisted he was correct. She then said yes, she had had five children but one had died. Compared with western doctors of about eighty years ago, Hay's diagnostic technique was phenomenal.

Around 1900-10, with the decline of the Chinese community, Doc Hay relied increasingly on his medical practice for his livelihood. The challenge was to move his medical practice from the dying Chinese community to the white community. This Hay was able to do, making him unique among Chinese herbal practitioners.

Hay's first patients, of course, were the Chinese who, like Lung On and himself, had come to the John Day area to mine. However, by the 1890s the placer mines were pretty well played out, so the Chinese workers began to work out as laborers on ranches and around the towns. Contact with whites, especially on the ranches, brought knowledge of Hay's medical expertise to the white community. Blood poisoning, or infection, was particularly troublesome for ranch hands, constantly around barbed wire and livestock.

In the 1880s, white doctors commended "laudable pus" which every healing wound was supposed to discharge. This mistaken belief, plus the long distances the injured had to travel and the usual reluctance of most people of those times to go to the doctor, meant that wounds were often severely infected by the time they received any attention. One old-timer, a ranch hand, got a bad infection on his ankle from a barbed wire wound and went to Doc Hay because a Chinese co-worker recommended Hay for treatment of blood poisoning. The ranch hand had to ride to John Day and the Kam Wah Chung and Co. Building in a wagon with his leg hanging over the side because it was too swollen and painful to bend. He said that he roomed in John Day for two days to take Hay's treatment, which consisted of drinking an herbal preparation three times a day. Hay had insisted that if he was to treat him, the ranch hand would have to agree to remain in town for the duration of the treatment; he did not want to treat someone and fail. Several patients have remarked on Hay's honesty and the fact that he would tell them if he could successfully treat an ailment or not.

Early in Doc Hay's practice, the Chinese often acted as intermediaries for white patients. In a letter dated January 1, 1897, a Lin Ying-ming wrote to Lung On and Doc Hay on behalf of a white friend. Hay had sent medicine for the person, but Lin Ying-ming, the Chinese intermediary, thought the price Hay had charged was too high. Lin went on to say, "Although the patient is a 'barbarian,' I am responsible for him. I don't think this practice is good for the future of your business." Obviously, the Chinese thought that perhaps Hay had two sets of prices, one for Chinese and one for whites.

Hay's big break into the white community came when he cured a prominent local rancher's son who had blood poisoning in a wound on his upper arm. Another rancher's wife, so the story goes, had advised the boy's desperate father to try the China doctor, as she had heard from the ranch hands that he could cure blood poisoning. Hay went out to the man's ranch to examine the boy. The boy had been treated by a western doctor, but his condition had worsened since. Hay told the distraught father that he could cure his son but the man would have to trust him implicitly. Also, the cure would cost a thousand dollars and would take six months. The father, well able to pay that amount, agreed to Hay's conditions.

Doc Hay stayed at that ranch for six days and nights watching over the boy. He immediately undressed the wound which, Hay said, had been packed incorrectly by the western doctor. He then proceeded to draw out the infection, using an ointment painted on the wounded arm with a feather. This ointment drew the infection until boils popped on the boy's arm. These boils were then drained of the poison. Hay also treated the boy with an herb preparation, which was continued after the six-day vigil. With the boy's recovery, Hay's reputation was established. Blood-poisoning treatment almost became Ing Hay's specialty.

Since Doc Hay could demonstrably cure blood poisoning

without resorting to operations, his success rate could not help being greater than that of other doctors around. People tend to evaluate a doctor by the extent and speed with which he can relieve their suffering and his ability to cure the disease or, at least, postpone death. Hay rated high in all of these areas.

But Hay did not break into practice among the local people without some opposition. Much of this opposition came from the very men he competed with in his medical practice. Old-timers state that the western doctors were rather jealous of Doc Hay's medical expertise. In addition to professional jealousy, there was also the issue of licensing, which came to a head in the medical profession in the United States between 1880-1910. By 1905, all but two states, Virginia and Maine, had joined the American Medical Association. Thus, perhaps the opposition to Hay was also a reflection of the local AMA attempting to extend some controls over medical practitioners in the John Day area just as local chapters of the organization were doing in other areas of the country.

In 1905, Ing Hay was charged by local white doctors with practicing medicine illegally, yet one eyewitness said that there was no jury in Grant County that would convict him. The respectable local community, at least, accepted Hay and Lung On and wanted them to remain. Hay's nephew says that Hay never worried about malpractice charges: "They'd never convict him anyway . . . they tried him, but he never done anything wrong. They couldn't get any man to stand up against him, so he had no fear."

Later that same year, Ing Hay received a letter from the State of Oregon saying that opium was to be used only as medicine and that he must keep careful records of his use of that drug. Perhaps his being Chinese had something to do with that admonition, plus the fact that, at least among people around John Day, Hay was known to be a user of opium himself. It is said, though, that sometime between 1906-10, Hay went to California and took the cure and never used opium again. Wing Wah stated that Hay just decided to quit opium and was able to because he had a remarkable will.

Like Hay, most doctors of that day had their own drugstores. An old horse-and-buggy doctor described western medical diagnostic techniques around 1902 by saying that what stuck out of the patients' shirts was looked at, their pulses counted if the doctor happened to have a watch, and then medicines were handed out from the stock on the shelves. One can understand how Doc Hay became such a noted doctor, considering the state of western medical technology and the lack of control of over-the-counter drugs.

Now an essential part of the community, Hay began to expand his herbal practice. Up to 1910, the herbal shop was not as important as the general store. But by 1910 the herbal invoices outnumbered general merchandise invoices. Hay became famous not only for blood poisoning treatment but also for cures for meningitis, lumbago, mumps, colds, stomach ailments, hemorrhaging, and influenza. It is said in the community that in the 1915 and 1919 flu epidemics none of Doc Hay's patients died. One woman stated that Hay successfully treated her, her mother, her aunt, and her brother during the first epidemic. Another brother in this same family was successfully cured of meningitis. As one person said, when talking of Hay's phenomenal treatment of meningitis: .

> The white doctors get ahold of 'em and they'd die, but this Chinaman would save them. He'd take a small white disc and go down the spine and all at once here would pop blood out of some place along the spine. Jim Polk is alive now and cured this way.

This is essentially the description all of Hay's former patients gave of his treatment for meningitis. Hay's nephew states that the practice of scraping the back is similar to acupuncture and its purpose is to increase the circulation. Most Chinese herbalists used a coin for this procedure. It was a part of any treatment that required revivifying nerves but not a complete treatment in itself.

It is important to note that the development of bacteriology did not begin in western medical technology until the mid-nineteenth century. Not until 1879 did Robert Koch discover the bacteria that caused wound infections. From a strictly medical point of view, bacteriology was the most important development of nineteenth-century medicine. Most fundamental bacteriological discoveries were made in Europe between 1878-87. These discoveries spread later to the United States. Yet these theories were not widely accepted until after the turn of the century. Dr. Arthur Hertzler, well-known American surgeon and writer, when recalling his practice in Kansas, noted that puerperal (childbirth) fever killed many women in his area. Further research revealed that this high incidence was linked to another doctor in the area who also raised hogs and did not hold to the practice of carefully washing his hands. It is an established medical tenet that the important factor in the prevention of infection of wounds is keeping the hands out of infectious material.

It was during this same period that the techniques of antisepsis and asepsis, in which all procedural instruments, the wound, and operator are sprayed with disinfectant, revolutionized surgical practices. The death rate from abdominal and pelvic surgery was forty percent in 1880-90 and fell below five percent by 1900.

Besides successful diagnosis and treatment of serious illness, Hay's practice was built on his unwillingness to resort to surgery. Most people between 1880-1920 were deathly afraid of the knife. Surgery was then at a primitive level. Also, many horse-and-buggy doctors practiced kitchen surgery—surgery in the patient's own home. The major disadvantages were the lack of assistants, clean surroundings, and a skilled anesthetist. Hay offered an alternative to people having to face the possibility of either primitive surgery at home or less-than-ideal surgery in hospitals in the area. A letter written to Hay in November of 1911 best expresses this concern:

> I was told that it was my heart and lungs and windpipe. There is a tumor on the left side of my neck. I would be so glad if you could reduce that as the doctors are wanting to cut it out and I have such a dread of the knife.

Hay offered hope to the desperate, and he would often take patients when conventional doctors had given up. One patient and friend said that Hay was independent and did not care if you doctored with him first or not. He would sometimes tell patients that they had better go see a conventional doctor because he could not cure them, and when the patients returned to him, worse than before, Hay would cure them. It is almost as if he wanted to test the patients' trust in him and then prove beyond a doubt that his treatment was superior to that of the other doctors.

People would continue to go to white doctors first, then would get so ill that in desperation they would go back to Hay. Hay seemed to like to take these patients and usually would end up saving their lives. Isolated people would write to him, describing horrible ailments and asking if he might cure them; they trusted his reputation as an honest doctor. One letter from Bend, dated July 10, 1904, is particularly poignant:

> Doctor Sir you bin [sic] reccomended [sic] as a first class doctor and as they is no doctor here that can do me any good I would like to know what you think about my case. I will tell you how I am and then if you can cure me I will come out there or you can send me medicine threw [sic] the mail. In your reply tell me what you will charge me. I am weak, have no appetite and suffer from sleeplessness. I have the whites, my hair is turning grey and falling out. I am 21 years old and have had this four years.

We do not have his reply.

Hay was one of the last horse-and-buggy doctors in the John Day area. Like other old-fashioned doctors, he became almost a part of the family. He would go to remote places to treat people and remain at their bedsides until their suffering was relieved. Unlike many old-time doctors, he could cure many fatal illnesses. He truly embodied the ideal of the immigrant who had come to stay. He brought his old country's training and skills to a new land and practiced the healing arts among a strange but, in the end, friendly people.

Doc Hay's following is as devoted today as it was when he was alive; he was a dedicated healer who genuinely wanted to help people. Speaking of his old uncle's practice, Hay's grand-nephew said, "I saw many a miracle." When asked if Hay ever talked about any of his cures, his nephew responded, "No, he was a typical professional and he never bragged about anything. One time a man wanted to write his story when he was alive but he said, 'No, I am remembered by my friends, that is enough for any man.' "

6.
The Golden Flower Blooms . . . .

Chinese is a subtle language, full of puns and literary allusions. The company name of Kam Wah Chung can thus be translated into English in several ways. The accepted one has been "The Golden Flower of Prosperity." For a period in the 1890s, while mining played out, railroads stalled, and the Chinese community grew ever smaller and less important, the name must indeed have seemed a cruel joke to Hay and Lung On. One by one, other Chinese firms with equally hopeful titles had disappeared. The two men must have spent many hours planning and worrying, fearing perhaps that one day they too would have to relocate—maybe back in China. Slowly, though, they made the crucial transition to a new economic base. Ing Hay succeeded in breaking into the white community with his medical practice and acquired his reputation as a China doctor who could work miracles after white physicians had dismissed difficult cases.

Lung On, and the Kam Wah Chung and Co. for which he was primarily responsible, underwent changes too. The many activities of the building narrowed and evolved. It became primarily the center for Ing Hay's medical practice, but it also became the headquarters of a small business empire which Lung On began to build.

The personal lives of the two men also evolved. Ing Hay, who had started as a rather traditional young miner, slowly became a respected professional, a sort of cross between an honored Confucian medical sage and a buggy-driving country doctor. As Hay acquired the respect of the surrounding community, his life became more and more fulfilling. He established patterns of behavior which he was to find satisfactory to the end of his days.

Lung On faced different problems. Had he stayed in China as the son of a wealthy and well-connected family, he could easily have moved into the very sort of upper-class status which Doc Hay later enjoyed. But Lung On left the Old World in search of adventure. During the 1890s and into the twentieth century, his energies led him in many different directions, including women.

One of the greatest obstacles to a full and satisfying social existence for Chinese men on the frontier was the absence of women. Less than ten percent of the immigrants were female, and the few marriageable women among them were highly prized. Quarrels and struggles over that small minority were frequent, as shown by the episode of Bong Gee's wives. Few Chinese women were equal to living the rough and culturally isolated life of the small frontier towns. "Crazy Jane" was a true exception who must have loved her husband very deeply to have remained. Most Chinese women found it far easier to locate in the large urban Chinese communities, where they could lead a more traditional life of relative ease and high status if they chose their husbands well. This left many Chinese males like Lung On isolated from feminine companionship unless they dared to establish ties with white women. Only the most courageous and confident did this.

There was some intermarriage between Chinese and whites in the nineteenth century, but it was unusual. When a case did occur, it was likely to become the subject of much public discussion. The tenor of these discussions can be seen in this article from the *Grant County News*, September 27, 1888: "Annie Tuttle, a fool girl in Brooklyn, was to have married a Chinaman last Wednesday, but the papers took it up and made so much talk that she bounced him."

When cases occurred closer to home, the local community was likely to be a little less obviously racist, but still an interracial couple met with obvious disapproval, as we see in this case from Albany, Oregon, reported in the same paper, February 21, 1889:

At Albany, Mrs. Jim Westfall, a descendant of Won Lung and a native worshipper at the shrine of Confucius, is attending the public schools and thereby creating an able-bodied kick from the parents and scholars.

Given the many years of anti-Chinese attitudes and the many barriers to understanding, there was a certain amount of danger to a Chinese who dared even talk to white women or girls. A near-tragedy was barely averted in The Dalles, Oregon, as reported in the *Grant County News* for May 23, 1889:

> A Chinaman arrested at The Dalles for assaulting a little girl came near being taken from the jail and hanged by the angry populace, and the mob assumed such huge proportions that two companies of the militia had to be quartered at the jail to prevent violence. As in nearly every case the first reports of a crime are exaggerated, and after the little girl and several witnesses testified that the Chinaman did not lay hands on her, he was turned loose.

Lung On was not content to remain an isolated adult male because he was a vital and active man in his prime. For him to have courted and married a local girl would have been risky enough. To acquire, as he did, the reputation of a local Lothario was downright dangerous. That Lung On did not hesitate to establish relations with a series of girls and women testifies to his courage. That he never seemed to have had any trouble at all with irate relatives, boy friends, or drunken cowboys testifies perhaps more to his strength. There are several stories of youths and adults from the local community teasing or, in some cases, attacking other Chinese, but Lung On was never approached nor spoken to save with the greatest respect. It is probable that Lung On's years of gambling and consorting with a fairly violent class of men gave him, and others, the knowledge that, like many men on the frontier, he could take care of himself if the need arose.

Markee Tom was a cook for a family in the Dayville area

who shared a similar interest in women. Sometimes he was called Monkey Tom by people in John Day, though not because he looked like a monkey but because of the play on words. Markee Tom was evidently educated and would correspond in Chinese with Lung On. To judge from Markee Tom's letters to Lung On, he shared the latter's remarkable success with women. Also, of all the Chinese, Markee Tom would have been the one most likely to have carried a gun, as he rode with American cowboys. It seems that Markee Tom was truly accepted by the white community, not only for his skill in riding and buckarooing but also because he lived in a white community away from most Chinese. It is only natural that Lung On and he would have had a friendship based on their mutual interests and abilities.

Lung On and his friend Markee Tom, who lived alone in the community of Dayville, called each other "oriental barbarians," a reference to the fact that they had taken on the dress and customs of Americans. Both spoke excellent English and entered business relations with whites on what appears to have been equal footing. Mixing freely with the Americans, they naturally came into contact with American women. Thus the two men were able to have friendships with these women without antagonizing the white males.

Ing Hay appears to have been the only person to object to these liaisons. In fact, according to eyewitnesses, Doc Hay would often get "hopping mad" at Lung On and his carefree ways. He would scold Lung On for spending too much time with women, away from the Kam Wah Chung and Co. Store. One person recalls that Lung On was not bad looking and says that women were always writing, inviting him to visit them. Apparently some of Lung On's female friends would contact him through Markee Tom. There is a series of letters in the Kam Wah Chung documents collection, written between 1905 and 1907, from Markee Tom to Lung On about various women.

One such letter, dated February 20, 1903, mentions a girl who wanted to see both of them again. In October of 1905, Markee Tom tells Lung On that she "wants Leon [Lung On] to come over, she is alone, her parents have left." This is the kind of invitation one could expect from a bored, liberated woman in the 1970s, but it is surprising to come across such a declaration at the turn of the century by a young woman still residing with her parents.

Another letter sent to Lung On by Markee Tom in October 1905 states, "There are two barbarian girls here, very nice, who do not look down on our Chinese. I think they will also like to meet Chen Shih since he is an Oriental barbarian too."

This letter alludes to the obvious racial tension people would feel about male-female friendships and acquaintances between Chinese males and local white females. Markee Tom's phrasing of this allusion is worth noting. He says that these girls "do not look down on our Chinese." Markee Tom sees the issue as one of others feeling or acting superior, not necessarily being racist. Also, he refers to "our Chinese" rather than "being Chinese." This is due perhaps to a feeling of separation or distinction from other Chinese since both Lung On and he were more adapted to western society than the other Chinese.

Later, in 1907, a Chinese, Ah Juck, wrote Lung On from Monument, Oregon, "Say, your girl friend is now working for my boss. Wouldn't you like to see her again? Why not come for a visit?"

These letters are merely suggestive of the wide range of friendships and liaisons Lung On enjoyed in the Grant County area. These friendships ranged from women enjoying Lung On's company and conversation to illicit meetings with a girl while her parents were away. These alliances between white women and Chinese males seem remarkable to us today because of our racist stereotype of Chinese males. The image of Chinese males on television and in the movies has been one of men either effeminate and sinister or cheerfully nonsexual. Markee Tom and Lung On fit neither of those caricatures.

There was more racial harmony on the frontier than we imagine today. Certainly from the examples of Markee Tom, Lung On, and Buckaroo Sam, we can see that integration was not uncommon in the male business world, in the more primitive world of the ranches and mines, and in the more personal world where men and women met. Both Lung On and Markee Tom had much to offer a lone woman in the West. Both were more cosmopolitan than many of the regular cowhands the women would meet in Eastern Oregon. Lung On was particularly desirable. He was known and respected from San Francisco to Seattle. He was well educated and could read and write in both English and Chinese. Lung On—or Leon, as many of his white friends called him—was a physical person too. He had come here to America first to mine but had prudently invested in a business and accumulated a small fortune. He had race horses and would travel with them, and he handled both saddle and carriage horses himself.

Being Chinese probably made Lung On more exotically attractive too. Since he was so Americanized, a woman could have the best of both worlds in one man. Probably Lung On had different attitudes toward a female than did the cowpokes she would meet. Most of the women mentioned in Markee Tom's letters were lower-class workers on ranches or in small communities in Eastern Oregon. Because, as a rule, Chinese women were not permitted to immigrate to the United States, a white woman who became friendly with a Chinese would, as a result of little competition, be highly valued. In addition, Lung On would sympathize with her complaints of put-downs and prejudice suffered as a minority worker in a predominantly white macho world. Lung On's tales of travels to big cities and faraway countries would widen the horizons of the world of a working woman in a time when only dire necessity gave a woman the opportunity to work. He would add interest and sparkle to what would have otherwise been a drab and dreary existence.

Lung On had another attraction for women. He was quite

generous and he grew quite wealthy. Under his intelligent, guiding hand, Kam Wah Chung and Co., the Golden Flower of Prosperity, began to bloom. Lung On brought many advantageous qualities to the business world. One of these was his courage, perhaps even his gambler's daring. Most Chinese businessmen were intensely conservative, trying to stay on well-worn paths of import-export or of small businesses serving a Chinese clientele. Lung On, on the other hand, was always quick to see a potential opportunity, and there is no evidence that anything to which he turned his hand did not prosper, save for an occasional loss at gambling. His major success was, of course, Kam Wah Chung and Co. itself. The building had begun as a social and commercial center for the Chinese and, before the period from about 1890 to 1900, its clientele was primarily Chinese. That it continued to exist until Lung On's death testifies to his business acumen.

Lung On was quick to see other opportunities as well. One of the major sources of his income was real estate. He bought land in many different areas. It is probable that he began speculating in mining areas, and then, as the economy diversified and stock raising and farming became more important, he too branched out. He began to buy property outside Oregon. There still exist records of transactions he made involving land in Washington and British Columbia. Some of the property was acquired from Chinese who were liquidating their investments prior to returning to China; other property was purchased from whites. The total of his investments in real estate cannot now be determined, but his safe-deposit box alone contained more than $44,000 in such holdings at his death.

Lung On had yet another advantage as a businessman: he had an open and innovative turn of mind. He was interested in all sorts of machinery and gadgets. As his adopted homeland went rushing into the twentieth century, with technical developments following each other rapidly, Lung On kept pace with it. Kam Wah Chung and Co. immediately bought each new patent device, whether for stamping checks, catching mice, or dispensing string. The Kam Wah Chung and Co. Building reportedly had one of the earliest telephones in the region.

He also invested on a larger scale. As the automobile was developed and the necessary system of roads built, he saw another opportunity. With a local white friend he invested in a small Pontiac dealership and service station, the "Tourist Garage." He thus became the first automobile dealer east of the Cascade Range in Oregon. The Tourist Garage prospered until his death in 1940. Lung On also learned to drive. There exist several pictures of the little Chinatown in the early twentieth century showing what we must assume was Lung On's personal car.

Lung On's investments also included stocks and bonds. He held large blocks of shares in all types of companies, from dairies to gold-mining ventures. In addition, he held many stocks in companies which folded during the depression of the 1930s.

From his many enterprises, Lung On, like Doc Hay, amassed a considerable fortune. By local standards, they were extremely well-to-do, although there were several local ranchers who were richer. By Chinese standards, though, they were wealthy indeed. Lung On owned many parcels of land scattered over an area greater than his home province of Kwangtung, which must have been about the bounds of his world as a young man. To own so much land was quite beyond the dreams of most Chinese. A man possessed of such wealth in traditional China could have engaged in ostentatious displays, hired servants, purchased concubines, oppressed his tenants, and used his wealth to avoid taxation. Lung On and Doc Hay did none of these things but lived simple and even frugal lives in John Day.

The building in which the two men lived out their lives today gives witness to their simple style of life. Doc Hay's bedroom was very small, less than eight by eight, and contained only a few crude items of furniture and, what must have been his pride, a brass bed frame. Lung On's bedroom is gone now (the space had to be converted into the museum store and curator's quarters) but it too was very small and crude, a converted storage room. The men dressed simply but well in western style suits and coats. We know that Doc Hay, like many older men, delighted in buying a new Stetson hat every few years. The two had a few expensive items of personal jewelry but did not engage in ostentatious display of their wealth.

To the local community of aging Chinese bachelors, Lung On was a source of steady support. We know that several of the Chinese depended directly upon his largesse for their support and that he was the man who buried the indigent and, in some cases, undertook the expense of sending their bones back to their families in China so that the ancestral cults might be carried on. These were, of course, all among his obligations as leader of the Sze Yup community.

Unfortunately, we cannot be sure just how important Lung On was outside the Grant County region. We do know that as the primary leader of the Sze Yup immigrants, he was the major figure among the Chinese who had emigrated into Eastern Oregon from those associated counties of Kwangtung province. We also know that he was only vaguely recognized as a man of importance in Portland, the urban center for Eastern Oregon Chinese, and that his fame did not extend as far north as Walla Walla, Washington, nor to Sand Point, Idaho. In those two areas he was regarded merely as Ing Hay's assistant.

During this period from about 1900 to 1939, while Doc Hay was building his medical reputation and his practice, and Lung On was pyramiding his investments, the two at some point were fully accepted by the local white community but were never absorbed by it. One indication of this is the desire of the two men to maintain contact with the old country itself, if not with their families.

China is an extraordinarily family-centered culture. The individual is not viewed as nearly so important as the family; traditional Chinese culture constantly reinforced the lesson that the individual should always view his own life, success, and happiness as second to that of the family. The older generations of grandfather and grandmother were absolutely dominant in the family as long as their health and wit permitted them to be at all active in its affairs. Marriages were arranged by the family to suit its needs, and the wishes of the individual were usually regarded as unimportant.

Both Lung On and Doc Hay grew up in this family structure, made arranged marriages, and started families. And each was an only son. This made them the center of their respective families. They were their families' sole link with its past, as the individual responsible for ancestor worship. They were also their families' sole hope for the future in that they alone were responsible for continuing the family line.

Under usual circumstances, such men would not have emigrated. The fact that they had started their own families doubtless made it somewhat easier, but still, it was unusual. The common pattern would have been for both men to stay in close contact with their parents, earn as much money as possible in the gold fields in a relatively short time, and then return to China to have other children and continue to build the family's joint fortune.

To the traditional Chinese way of thinking, Lung On and Doc Hay proved very poor sons. As family-centeredness is the primary Confucian virtue, both were traitors to their families and their culture. They wrote only infrequently, rarely sent money home, and finally, never returned.

Both families responded to their absent sons' neglect by bringing as great a pressure as was possible from many thousands of miles away. This meant primarily a series of angry and pleading letters and attempts to have other family members make the same arguments. Lung On received one such letter from his father in July of 1899:

> Come home as soon as you can. Don't say no to me any more. You are my only son. You have no brothers and your age is near forty . . . . We need you, you must come home . . . .

Come back, let our family be reunited and enjoy the remainder of our life. Your father.

                                                        Chu-Chia

In September 1901, he received a similar letter from his daughter:

> Father, you have been overseas for so long that you must have made much money. But I think constantly that I have never seen my Father. Last year we all thought that you might come home, but our hopes were dashed. Father, we have not heard from you in four years . . . Please return as soon as possible and our whole family can be reunited. Your unfilial daughter,
>
>   Guey-sim.

In March 1905, he received a letter from his cousin:

> Two years ago your mother passed away. Last year your daughter married. Your aged father is paralyzed. He will pass away soon. Your wife feels neglected. The neighbors are moved by her melancholy and ill-fortune. Come back as soon as you receive this. If you don't return, you should send money home for your family's expenses. Your cousin.
>
>   Liang Kwang-jan.

Doc Hay received similar letters from the members of his family. Because his wife had given birth to a son after he left China, there was less pressure to return to take up the ancestral cults, and the future of that branch of the Ing family was assured. But since he did have a son, his refusal to send money for support of the family was even more shocking to the traditional Chinese mind, which held sons in very high esteem and had little regard for daughters. Ing Hay's father wrote him in May of 1903:

> You have been away for more than ten years. Men go abroad so that they might make money for support of their families, but

you have sent neither money nor a letter since you left . . . . Do you intend to let us starve? . . . . You think only of yourself and enjoy your solitary life with no thought for us. This is not suitable for a moral man.

Despite this constant pressure, the two men continued to have little contact with their families in China and never did send any meaningful amounts of money to them. By traditional Chinese standards, both classic examples of selfish and thoughtless prodigal sons. However, to Doc Hay and Lung On, it seemed quite different—their cultural values had simply changed. They did not regard the old Chinese reasons for returning or sending money as compelling.

Ing Hay and Lung On did keep other ties with China. They were ardent patriots and eagerly followed political and social developments in their homeland. Among the Kam Wah Chung and Co. papers are receipts which indicate that the two frequently contributed to progressive political organizations in China. They supported Sun Yat-sen's efforts to overthrow the Manchu monarchy and create a modern republic. Sun Yat-sen, the "Father of the Chinese Republic," was in some regards himself an Overseas Chinese. He toured through the United States several times before the successful revolution against the Manchus in 1911-12. For a brief period Sun was the president of the new country, but he was forced out of China by the war lords. Sun financed his own revolutionary activities in the period before 1911 in large part with the contributions of Overseas Chinese communities in the United States. He toured the United States with the assistance of local lodges of the Chee Kung Tang in 1904 and again in 1908 and 1910. Several of our older Chinese witnesses tell us that at some point, either in 1904 or 1910, Sun visited Portland, and possibly Pendleton.

Ing Hay and Lung On were both active in raising funds for Sun's efforts, and if indeed he did visit that city, they probably went to Pendleton to see him. Another witness, George Lee, remembers that the Portland community was quite split in its support of Sun, and many members of it still saw the Manchu dynasty as China's legitimate government. That Ing Hay and Lung On did support him so ardently testifies to their modernity. Even during the chaos of the war-lord period, from about 1916 to 1927, the two men continued to send some funds to China. In the Kam Wah Chung papers is a certificate which indicates that they gave a substantial sum to Yen Hsi-shan, the so-called Model War Lord of North Central China.

The values of Ing Hay and Lung On had clearly changed. They had acquired progressive, modern values. They would support a political reformer like Sun Yat-sen or a centralizer like Yen Hsi-shan, but they would not respond to the appeals of a traditional Confucian father demanding their obedience. However, there is another important factor—the two were in effect cut off from China by American immigration laws.

Whether or not Doc Hay was an illegal immigrant, the confusion of the American immigration laws was such that any sensible Chinese immigrant, legal or illegal, would avoid the attention of the authorities. Because he was a substantial citizen, there was little danger of Hay's falling afoul of immigration in Portland or Eastern Oregon, but to return to China and then re-enter the United States might have been very difficult, if not impossible. Many thousands of Chinese were in China with valid American re-entry permits in 1888, when the law was changed and they were denied re-entry. After that, Chinese immigrants had little faith in the American government's word on immigration matters. Expecially in the period before about 1930, Lung On and Ing Hay would have feared that if they returned to China it would have been impossible to return. By the time such fears became less important, their parents were dead, their children grown and married, and the ties to the old society had decayed to the point where they had no desire to take them up again.

As the ties to family in China grew less important, the two acquired family ties in this country. Ing Hay always had a circle of relatives here—some cousins, others more distant—and was able to call upon them in time of need. Although Lung On had fewer relatives in Eastern Oregon than Ing Hay, he had correspondingly closer ties in the local white community.

In October of 1902, a white family that had moved from Prairie City to John Day was unable to find a house "uptown," so they rented one down in Chinatown. The family got to know Lung On and Doc Hay very well. Two of the children, a boy and girl, became very close to Lung On, who became almost a member of the family. The boy, four or five years old at the time, would hang around the store. (He now tells of once riding out to Fox Valley with Lung On and Doc Hay when they were called out to treat the boy's sick relative.) The girl, only two months old when she moved to Chinatown, recalls that both Doc Hay and Lung On would pick her up and she would call them "Daddy," which delighted them both.

Although the Chinese did not seem to have much of a sweet tooth, nor did they like milk products, Lung On had acquired a taste for both. As any friendly neighbor might, he took to calling on the children's family just to visit and would pop his head through the doorway and ask, "You got some cake? You got some cream?" He would then sit and visit and the family would serve him a sweet.

When the girl graduated from high school, Lung On presented her with a diamond ring. After she married and had her own family, Lung On took to stopping by her home with the old request, "You got any cake? You got some cream?" It appears that she became for him a sort of granddaughter or niece, one who would welcome him into the warmth of a family circle, feed him a treat, and just talk for a while.

In later years, when Lung On was ill, the girl nursed him. She would take him his breakfast, clean his false teeth, and make him comfortable. Then in the evening she and her husband would bring him his dinner before they themselves ate. Lung On had truly found a family of his own here in the United States. In gratitude to the small child who remained his friend, he gave her another, larger diamond. She says Lung On was one of the best friends she ever had.

The part of regular family life which the two men missed most was having small children of their own. Among the many items they regularly saved at the Kam Wah Chung and Co. were pictures of children. Some of these pictures were cut from calendars, others from advertisements and newspapers, and each was put away safely in an envelope or box. The people of John Day who were children in the 1920s and 1930s today remember the old Chinese community with special fondness because they were always welcome at feasts or celebrations, and every child who entered the Kam Wah Chung and Co. store was given a piece of candy or an exotic fruit.

The changing attitude toward Chinese holidays and festivals provides a somewhat ironic measure by which to assess the evolution of local white regard for the Chinese minority. In the period before about 1890, Chinese festivals, particularly the Lunar New Year, were a constant source of ridicule, amusement, and, sometimes, anxiety. The large and noisy Chinese celebrations drew curious onlookers. A local newspaper report indicates the attitude toward Chinese celebrations, "Saturday was a China day of large dimensions. Many swine were slain for the occasion." (*Grant County News*, September 18, 1884.)

In a story on the Lunar New Year, February 25, 1886, the *News* write, "Last Thursday the residents of Chinatown down the river [settled] up their Josh monkey business for this year by all getting Drunk . . . . " But, by the 1920s, the celebration of the Lunar New Year in Chinatown had become a local holiday for which all schools were let out so that the children might attend. Without exception, everyone interviewed who lived in John Day or Canyon City as a child remembered the holiday and remarked upon it with nostalgic pleasure.

One person interviewed said he rarely ever missed a New Year's celebration in John Day's Chinatown. He recalled:

All the Chinese men were there as a rule and they always

roasted a hog, a big hog, and had a barbecue pit dug down in the ground. They set off lots of firecrackers and bombs. Right down the main street of town [Chinatown] they had big high poles with strings of firecrackers hanging down. When they started that, they never let up, oh, for a couple of hours, and it was just a continual popping of firecrackers there, and ever once in a while they'd set off one of these bombs and people would come from all over, and there were buckets of tea and roast duck.

There was more white people there than Chinese, and then of a night, after this celebration was all over they had a great big room where there was gambling and long tables in there, and they'd invite all their main friends from all over the country to come and serve this pig and then what was left they would slice it up in slices and give it to their friends around—boy, it was really good, it was delicious—nothing better.

Yeah, that was the time . . . the firecrackers . . . all the kinds would go to every little shack and they'd all have something on Chinese New Year's. Oranges . . . like those peanut kisses always a favorite with all the kids . . . . [Owyhee Peanut Kisses, made right in Eastern Oregon, are a frequently remembered treat given people as children by the Chinese]

And instead of going to this joss house, on Chinese New Year's they'd go right in there to Leon's place . . . . I've seen 'em a lot of times, and get right down on their knees right in front of that [altar] in that back room back in there . . . and they'd get down and worship. I've seen them do that; on Chinese New Year's . . . that's the only time they ever did it.

A relative of Hay's, recalling John Day's Chinatown, mentioned that the school was close to the Kam Wah Chung and Co. Building. He said that on Chinese New Year's, when the firecrackers were set off, school had to be let out because the school officials could not keep the children in.

The friendly attitude of Lung On and Ing Hay toward children and the special pleasure both seem to have taken in their presence indicate that, however hardhearted and unfilial they must have seemed to their family back in China, they very much missed the regular family ties which conditions in the United States denied them.

The two men had also established other ties here. Lung On always had the company of other men, gambling, or travelling. Doc Hay became an active member of the local Masons and had a Mason's funeral at his death in 1952. Some Chinese, like Sun Yat-sen, have insisted that the Masons were very similar to Chinese secret societies; indeed, Sun implied ties between them. Hay must have found the Masons an especially congenial group because of his love of ritual.

It is impossible to say to what exact degree Lung On and Ing Hay were assimilated into American life and into the local community of John Day. Neither is it particularly crucial that we try to do so.

The importance and the contribution of Ing Hay and Lung On to the community gave it a very favorable view of Chinese, which continues to this day. We interviewed several younger Asian-Americans who came in and grew up in John Day in the 1950s and 1960s, after Hay and Lung On had created their legends, and none of them could think of a single racial incident or prejudicial action on the part of any member of the community, though each mentioned incidents involving strangers to the community who came in temporarily from outside.

7.
. . . . And Fades

Early in 1940, Lung On was taken ill. Though he had been an extremely healthy man who was rarely ill, after a brief period of increasingly serious symptoms, he died in April. The nature of the illness remains a mystery. So quickly had it come on and so swiftly had he died that some of the townspeople, who did not know the little Chinese community well, hinted darkly that he had been poisoned. It is possible that he had been terminally ill for some time and Ing Hay and he had concealed the fact from friends to spare their feelings. Hay must have been heart-broken that despite the many medical miracles he had worked he was unable to help his friend and partner.

Lung On was sixty-eight at his death and had made adequate legal preparations for his demise. He left an estate worth almost ninety thousand dollars, a remarkable figure for a non-professional living in such a small town. The entire estate went to Doc Hay for use during his lifetime, with stipulations that half the estate then go to his daughter back in China at Hay's death.

In making these provisions for his daughter, Lung On showed a belated concern for his family in China, this special bequest was never to be honored. By the time of Hay's death in 1952, China had again gone through upheavals which were to affect its relations with the United States. Chinese immigrants and American-born Chinese were to be cut off from their ancestral homeland for some time. After the 1948-49 victory of the Communist Party, led by Mao Tse-tung against the American ally, Chiang K'ai-shek, the United States attempted to make China an international outlaw. Using her immense economic power and political influence, the United States succeeded in keeping China out of the mainstream of international relations and recognized the refugee Chiang regime on Formosa as the legitimate government of mainland China. The anti-Communist tensions of the Cold War and the state of enmity resulting from the Korean War further increased tensions between the two countries. When Doc Hay died in 1952, relations between China and the United States were at their lowest point in history.

After his death, the caretakers of Lung On's estate were obliged to find his daughter, Lung Guey Sim, and give her the remainder of the estate, which had been sadly depleted by legal expenses and unauthorized use by the executor. Unfortunately, the Cold War had almost paralyzed communication between China and the United States. Obstacles to the transfer of funds were enormous.

The years immediately after the establishment of the Communist government in China were very hard ones. Successive years of bad crops, the dislocation caused by long years of war between Japan and China, and then the civil struggle between the Communists and the Nationalists of Chiang K'ai shek made life extremely difficult. Lung Guey Sim knew of her father's death and of the terms of his will, and she wrote several times, pleading for the money to be disbursed. One such letter gives us a feeling of the acute need which she had for the money:

> Mr. Executor: My life is completely in your hands. I beseech you to quickly send me the money. Save my life. Not only me but my whole family will thank you. My father, Lung On, now in Heaven, will thank you. Please quickly send me the money. [Another member of his family added the following note to the letter:]

> Lung Guey Sim lives with a daughter-in-law in the country. Because of a lack of money two girls [in that family] were sick and died last month . . . . We have kept Lung Guey Sim from knowing this. Otherwise she would be heartsick. God in Heaven knows of these matters.

Several of the addresses which Lung Guey Sim used while pursuing her father's estate were in Hong Kong, and a few times she appeared to testify before British Crown colonial authorities there. It is possible that Lung Guey Sim was, in fact, a citizen of Hong Kong and not an enemy alien at all. Whatever the facts, the situation was impossible and she never received the remaining portion of the estate, which eventually passed into the control of the State of Oregon since no legitimate claimant could be found.

In a way, the "China doctor" died with Lung On. While the outside world saw only Ing Hay's importance, and it was Ing Hay who had the specialized medical knowledge, the "China doctor" was truly a blending of the talents and personalities of Ing Hay and Lung On. After Lung On's death, the medical practice was never the same. Of the two men, Lung On clearly made the best adaptation to the American West. Ing Hay was honored and respected, but Lung On was a full participant and in his person bridged the gap from a raw country exploited for its mineral wealth to a settled culture of ranchers, loggers, and small businessmen like Lung On himself.

Lung On's grave, on a hill overlooking the valley in which John Day and the Kam Wah Chung and Co. Building are nestled, testifies to his dual nature. In English are his name and dates; in Chinese characters, his place of origin in China.

One of the most striking images which has emerged from our interviews at John Day, Canyon City, and Prairie City is the one which we heard from several older members of the white community. They said that in the "old days" whenever the Chinese ventured out from Chinatown into the white business district, they inevitably walked single file with Lung On in the lead. The picture of the short line of aging bachelors led by Lung On, ready to interpret or turn away trouble, is a symbolic representation of his importance to the Chinese community and to his place in it. One wonders where they might have been without him, or if they could even have remained in the area without his assistance.

Ing Hay was hard hit by his friend's death. They had been together for fifty-three years. He was not only Ing Hay's skilled translator and chauffeur but his last link with Old China, and with the frontier of the gold camps and boom towns to which they had each been drawn as youths. By 1940, Doc Hay's eyesight was all but gone, and with his partner dead, it is hard to imagine what loneliness must have beset him in the old Kam Wah Chung and Co. Building, which had once been the scene of so much noisy ceremony and of a friendship which spanned two eras and two cultures.

Hay was genuinely worried that without Lung On he himself would not be as welcome in the community. He went to see Lung On's special friend, the girl, now a woman, whose family Lung On had taken in when they could find no other place to live. Feeling lost and isolated, he told that woman that he feared the "white man" was crooked. He told her that now that Lung On was gone, he feared she probably would not come around to see him any more, but she did continue to go down to the dark, old building to visit with the last Chinese, left alone in the once-crowded Chinatown of John Day.

Ing Hay had no immediate relatives but there was a family with members in both Portland and Idaho who were related. They sent a newphew, E. B. Wing, himself a herbal practitioner who was living and working in Portland, to his aid. He found Ing Hay extremely upset. As E. B. Wing related, "He said, 'My partner's gone, I won't have long to live.' He just gave up; he didn't want to live. He was practically blind and his partner was gone." E. B. Wing contacted his brother, Bob Wah, also an herbal doctor, who was practicing in Idaho. Bob Wah then moved to John Day to live and work with Ing Hay and the old man's spirits soon improved.

Bob Wah, his wife Rose, and their four children—Bob Jr., Eddie, Henry and Lillian—all loved the old man and took him into their family. For the first time since he had seen his father off for China in 1887, Ing Hay had a family relationship. He continued to live in the old Kam Wah Chung and Co. Building but took most of his meals with the Wah family in the house they bought right across what had once been the main street of the old Chinatown and which was now Canton Street, John Day.

With his new family and his old friends, Doc Hay recovered some of his early vigor. He became a sort of honored elder in the community, always glad to see an old friend or meet a new one. It was said that occasionally he would meet a person whom he had not seen in decades and had known only briefly, but so sharp were his senses that he could instantly recognize them from their voices and call them by name.

He delighted in small jokes and pranks with friends and with local children. He had one trick that he played on several people. With little eyesight left, he had to hold an object very close to distinguish its color and general shape. Most people thought him stone blind. He would sometimes maintain that he could tell a flower's color by its smell. A disbelieving child or adult would unsuspectingly bring him a flower to test him, and when he held it close, inhaling deeply of its fragrance, he could make out the color. After a brief period of pretended puzzlement, he would correctly announce its color, leaving the victim muttering about the special powers of the old herbal doctor.

As, he grew older, he had to give up some of his lifelong pleasures. He had always been a man who liked a social drink with friends, but he stopped this. Old friends, not knowing his new regimen, would often give him a good bottle of Scotch, but he would pass it on to other friends who would drink it. One of his special pleasures had been cigars. He had smoked cigars constantly for a very long time, but in the late 1940s he fell asleep, with a lighted cigar, in the old red chair in which he used to sit while feeling a patient's pulse for diagnostic purposes. The cigar smoldered, then set fire to the chair and his clothing. After he woke and, with the aid of the Wahs, put out the small fire, he announced: "I'm going to quit smoking. I don't mind dying naturally but I'm not going to burn to death in a chair." His announcement was met with a certain amount of scepticism since he had smoked for so long, but just as he gave up the opium habit earlier, he now stopped smoking immediately and finally.

Doc Hay never lost interest in his profession. With both Bob Wah and his other nephew, Bob's brother, E. B. Wing, he would occasionally stay up all night talking about the special properties of herbs and difficult medical cases he had seen in his long career. E. B. Wing recalled:

> One night I talked to him half the night . . . . Herbs were about the only thing we would talk about. He would never brag about cases unless some friend came in to visit him: "You remember me? I'm so-and-so, remember me? I had pneumonia, I had the flu, I had the Rocky Mountain spotted fever and you cured me."

With Bob Wah's assistance, Ing Hay began in 1941 to practice once more. Things were not the same though. Attitudes toward medical care had changed. People no longer trusted herbal physicians, thinking they were no better than quacks and preferring rather to go to one of the many young and newly trained conventional physicians who had moved into the area. Ing Hay seems also to have feared malpractice suits or being charged with practicing without a license, which had happened so often in the old days. Perhaps he thought that, without Lung On's circle of friends and his aid, new law cases might have less happy outcomes than the old ones which had always resulted in his acquittal as some member of the jury eagerly testified to his skills. He did see some older patients and Bob Wah tried to take over the practice. Hay's last patient book records his patients from 1938 until 1942. Primarily he mailed out old herbal preparations to long-time patients who had been taking them for several years.

Bob Wah and Ing Hay both faced a new problem, however. From the time of the beginning of the second Sino-Japanese War in 1937, China had been in turmoil and the medicinal herbs which they had formerly imported from China by way of

Seattle and San Francisco became harder and harder to get. The two looked around for substitute sources but found the herbs inadequate. Herbs raised in a climate different from the hot, semi-tropical one of the Canton area lacked strength. As E. B. Wing, himself familiar with this problem, recalled:

> Doc Hay said it was no use. With the old herbs, you could use two or three ounces in a prescription and that was sufficient. With the new herbs from different parts, why, you had to put a pound in."

Despite the problems in re-establishing the practice after Lung On's death, the little Chinese community in John Day grew for a short period. Bob Wah and Ing Hay sponsored other Chinese-Americans into the community, including distant relatives and friends. One such family which included several children, ran a successful restaurant before moving on to Pendleton and eventually to Portland.

Bob Wah's children grew older and moved away to go to college, build professional careers, and establish families of their own. Bob's wife, Rose, died and he remarried a woman named Lily, whose fate it was to be the last member of the John Day Chinatown.

Then, in 1948, Doc Hay fell while alone in the Kam Wah Chung and Co. Building and broke his hip. This was the first time he had been ill with a malady which he could not treat himself, and he did not trust conventional western medicine. He probably remembered the old days when doctors had often been no better than butchers. He also knew of the countless cases he had saved after other doctors had brought them to the brink of death through incorrect or inadequate treatment. Bob Wah and E. B. Wing, who came in from Portland to help, anxiously thought of a way to help him.

Living in the community was a western physician whom Hay had known from the time this physician was a small child. Hay trusted this man and he examined Hay, telling him that he had to go into a hospital to have a pin inserted in his broken hip.

Now a new problem arose. Hay was convinced of the need for the pin, but he refused to ride in an ambulance. He was a superstitious man and would not relax in a vehicle which had carried so many dead and dying spirits. E. B. Wing and another good friend of Hay, Cliff Benson, borrowed a station wagon and took him to the hospital in Portland. His leg was set, although it never really healed, and he went into a nursing home in Portland where he could get proper care.

Doc Hay lived in the nursing home for four years, bedridden. He was always eager to see old friends from John Day and many came over whenever possible to visit him. His closest friend during this period was his nephew, E. B. Wing. The fractured hip, however, never really healed and Ing Hay was under constant treatment. He was even subjected to a long series of X-rays. One wonders what the old doctor, whose own powers had always come from nature's herbs and his own highly developed sense of touch, thought of the machines which could see into his very bones. He had been in the nursing home four years, when, in the fall of 1952, he was left untended for some time on a cold metal table during one such series of X-rays. He caught pneumonia and died.

There is more than a little irony in the manner of his death. There is no evidence that the hospital or the attending physicians were negligent. What killed Ing Hay was, of course, basically his own advanced age, but the immediate cause was a system of medicine which all too often had ceased to care for patients as people but to see them as "cases" which could be cured by some application or other of "science." In pursuit of this scientific cure, Ing Hay lay old and chilled under the snout of the giant X-ray machine, on the sterile steel table, and he died. His own patients had often come to him in the advanced stages of gangrene, or suffering from a mysterious fever, or a common disease like Rocky Mountain spotted fever, or typhoid, and they had been quickly cured by this old man who could feel their pulse and give them a bitter but healing herbal concoction. This same old man caught his fatal chill sandwiched unfeelingly between chrome and plastic.

And so Ing Hay died at the age of eighty-nine. He left a very small estate, only several thousand dollars. This small estate shows the decline of the store and the herbal medical practice after the death of Lung On, but it also shows Hay's generosity. In his old bed in the Kam Wah Chung and Co. Building, the heirs and friends who cleaned up after his death found more than twenty-three thousand dollars in uncashed checks from patients. Bob Wah had known that Hay had not been cashing the checks and had asked him why. According to one witness, Hay replied, "[They are all] good people. I don't need the money, I no cashee. They need it." Doc Hay had put the interests of his friends and patients ahead of those of his distant relatives who would eventually inherit his estate. It is a remarkable testimony to the degree to which he had become a part of the community.

In 1955, Bob Wah deeded the Kam Wah Chung and Co. Building to the city of John Day as Ing Hay had instructed, with the provision that the building be made into a museum, a monument to the contribution of the Chinese community of John Day to the development of Eastern Oregon. For many years nothing was done. After the successive changes of city administration and the deaths of legal executors, the city soon lost all awareness of its actual ownership of the building. During this period it remained shuttered and locked, and the thousands of artifacts remaining from the Chinese mining community, Lung On's and Hay's personal items, herbal medicines, priceless antiques, books in Chinese and English, calendars decades old, all remained in the dark, perfectly preserved by the even temperatures of the old stone building and the dry cold of Eastern Oregon.

Bob Wah died in 1966. His second wife, Lily, lived in John Day for a few years before she moved away to San Francisco. Only the old Kam Wah Chung and Co. Building remained, mute witness to the once bustling John Day Chinese community.

In 1967, while surveying the land around the Kam Wah Chung to develop a city park, the city of John Day found that it owned the Kam Wah Chung Building and its contents. Professional assistance from the National Trust for Historic Preservation, the Oregon State Parks Bureau, the Oregon Historical Society, and students and faculty from the University of Oregon and Lewis and Clark College all combined with community volunteers and financial donors to rebuild the building, clean and inventory its contents, and replace them as they had been in 1940, just before the death of Lung On.

The Kam Wah Chung and Co. Building and its contents are the greatest single surviving group of original materials dating from the nineteenth-century influx of Chinese immigrants into the American West. Locked behind its stone walls is the entire history of the Chinese community of John Day—and the life stories of Lung On and the China Doctor.

APPENDIX
Sixty-two Chinese Herbs and Medications

This Appendix is intended as a sample listing of some of the more than five hundred different herbs and medications found in Doc Hay's collection inside the Kam Wah Chung and Co. Building. The Chinese name is given first, using the Wade-Giles romanization; then the Latin name is given and when possible, the common name. A brief description of its properties follows, along with some of the diseases or conditions for which it was commonly used.

It is important to remember that most often these herbs and medications were used in concert with ten to twenty others, not uncommonly with herbs having completely opposite properties and effects. This was done purposely by the Chinese herbalist to introduce a balance into the diseased—or in the Chinese doctor's eyes—the physically unbalanced patient.

The list would have been impossible to compile without Dr. Kaihua Ger's patient diligence in deciphering the aged characters identifying the herbs and then searching for their Latin names, after which he found descriptive definitions of their medical uses.

The categories into which the sixty-two herbs and medications have been divided are arbitrary. All have several properties and are used in many ways for various ailments. By categorizing them into groups, we have attempted to make a limited amount of information about Doc Hay's treatments accessible to the general reader.

For further reading on Chinese medicine, these two books may be helpful: *Traditional Medicine in Modern China* by Ralph C. Croizier (Harvard University Press, 1968), and *Chinese Herbal Medicine* by C. P. Li (U.S. Department of Health, Education, and Welfare, HEW Publications No. N/H 75-732, 1974).

Familiar Herbs and Medications:
1. Pai-pu. *Stemona tuberosa.* Wild Asparagus

   The roots of this plant are used in medicine. In the market, the herb appears in the form of brown, dried, shrivelled pieces, two to four inches long. It is prescribed as a cough remedy, to expel gas, as a vermifuge, and as an insecticide.

2. Fu-ling. *Pachyma cocos.* Tuckahoe, Indian Bread

This a fungus which grows upon the roots of fir trees. The Chinese use it for both food and medicine. As medicine it appears in the form of large tubers with corrugated blackish-brown skins. The herb has no taste or smell and is considered an aid to digestion, a nutrient, a diuretic, and sedative. It is often prescribed for nervous disorders in children and for wasting diseases.

3. Tsang-erh-tzu. *Xanthium strumarium.* Cocklebur

The Chinese use the leaves of this common weed as food and dye. Medicinally, the fruits are regarded as slightly deleterious. They are used as a tonic, anti-rheumatic, anti-periodic, and diuretic remedy. Cooling and quieting properties are ascribed to the shoot and leaves. These are considered to be astringent and hemostatic. The flowers are often prescribed to treat colds.

4. Yu-li-zen. *Prunus japonica.* Dwarf Flowering Cherry

A small tree, six to seven feet in height, it bears small, red cherry-like fruit. The fruit has a rather harsh, sour taste. The kernels of the fruit stones, dried or mixed with honey, are used in medicine. They are regarded as having demulcent, diuretic, soothing properties. It is prescribed for rheumatism, fevers, stomach pains, indigestion, and constipation. Mixed with Baroos camphor, it is given for conjunctivitis.

5. Peng-sha. Borax

This white crystalline salt has disinfectant, preservative, and diuretic properties. It is used as an aid to menstruation and to suppress coughs and to promote a flow of saliva. Externally, it is applied to the inflamed parts of the mouth, throat, and the eyes.

6. Ding-shiang. *Jambosa caryophyllus.* Clove

The fruits of the plant are used in medicine. It is recommended in the treatment of cholera, pain in the abdomen, colic, and dyspepsia. The herb is also believed to have peptic and aphrodisiac properties.

7. Chi-nei-chin. *Galli Corium stomachichum.* Chicken Gizzards

This herb is derived from dried chicken gizzards. Internally, they are used for dyspepsia, dysmenorrhoea, nausea and vomiting. By mixing the powdered gizzards with oil, the drug is applied to abscesses.

8. Pai-tou-kou. *Amomum cardamomum.* Siam Cardamon

This round cardamom originates in the East Indies. The seeds are mainly used in medicine. They are prescribed for heartburn, vomiting, pulmonary diseases, debility, ague, and for hangovers.

9. Ching-pi. Citrus

This is the peel of an unripe orange. The herb is considered cooling, thirst-relieving, stomachic, and carminative.

10. La-jiao. Capsicum, Red Pepper

The Chinese regard red peppers as a stimulant to the digestion and as a vermifuge. They are recommended for edema and cold dissipation.

Exotic Herbs and Medications:

1. Shis-jue-ming. *Haliotidis concha.* Abalone

This is a kind of sea shell. When dried, it is used in medicine. The herb is prescribed for eye diseases, fevers due to tuberculosis, headache due to high blood pressure, diuresis, and gonorrhoea.

2. Shih-hui. Calcium Oxide, Lime

This is a white substance obtained by the action of heat on limestone shells, and other material containing calcium carbonate. It is poisonous. As medicine, Shih-hui is primarily used as a preservative, purulent, and anti-worming agent.

3. Wei-pi. *Erinacei corium*

This is the dried skin of an animal resembling the rat. It has styptic property. The drug is given for hemorrhoids, seminal flux, bleeding of the uterus, intestinal bleeding, ulcers, and inflamed mammary glands in women.

4. Ren-chung-pai. *Calamitas urinae hominus*

This is the dried white substance derived from urine. Boiled with ginseng, the drug is said to have aphrodisiac and sedative properties. It is given in the treatment of sores in the mouth, some children's diseases involving cartilage and as a disinfectant when applied to abscesses, gumboils and eczema.

5. Da-guei-ban. *Geoclemys reveesii, Testudinis carapax*

This is a tortoise shell. The Chinese use it for its so-called tonic, aphrodisiac qualities. It is used to treat bleeding hemorrhoids, bleeding in the uterus, cartilage diseases in children, and general debility.

6. Shih-shieh.

   This is a variety of crab. It is mainly used to treat eye diseases, especially metallic poisonings.

7. Hu-gu. Tiger's bone

   The Chinese believe that tiger's bone can ward off evil influences. They also consider it sedative and antispasmodic and helpful to the bones. This drug is sometimes applied as a plaster to dog bites and severe burns.

8. Wu-ling-chih. *Pteropi excrementum*

   This is the guano of a variety of nightingale and it has a very bad odor. It is useful in treating dysmenorrhoea, colic, wasting diseases in children, uterine bleeding, and snake, centipede, and scorpion bites.

Herbs used to Treat Wounds, Abscesses and Sores:

1. Tung-kuei-tze. *Abutili semen, Abutillon indicum*

   The leaves, roots, and seeds of the plant are used in various medicines. The seeds resemble those of the elm. They are recommended in stomach and intestinal ailments, and in mineral poisons. Due to their muscilaginous qualities, the seeds are also used to lubricate the body passages and to make natal labor easier. Besides its uses as a diuretic and thirst-quenching remedy, the root is sometimes administered in treating gangreous wounds. The ash is employed as a styptic in wounds, also.

2. Shih-wei. *Polypodum lingua*

   This is a plant with leathery leaves and is found growing on rocks and old brick walls. The dried leaves are considered to be diuretic and tonic. They are prescribed in the treatment of wounds, boils, and for urinary difficulties and kidney stones. The drug is also thought to be useful in cooling the blood and in promoting the excretion of water.

3. Sheng-pa-tou. *Croton tiglium.* Croton

   This is a small, three-celled, and triangular-like fruit with a yellowish-brown color. It is poisonous and has a very acrid taste. The fresh fruits, the oil, the testa, and the root of the tree are all used in medicine. The herb's uses are varied, including treatment of colds, fevers, diarrhoea and dysentery, and in delayed menstruation. It is also recommended in apoplexy, paralysis, toothache, and throat infections. Externally it is used in combination with rapeseed oil for various kinds of skin infections. The testa is recommended only for discharges, while the bruised root is applied to abscess and cancerous sores.

4. Hu-huang-lien. *Barkhausia repens, Picrorrhiza kurrooa*

    This shooting plant resembles that of *Brunella vulgaris*. The dried roots which are used in medicine are irregular, contorted pieces. The drug has tonic, astringent, antiperiodic properties. It is used in weakening and wasting diseases of children, Kan diseases in Chinese, and for dysentery. Mixed with goose gall, it is most often applied to cancerous sores and hemorrhoids.

5. Liu-ji-nu-tsao. *Senecio palmatus*

    The plant has hairy leaves, a red stem, and yellow flowers. The stalk and leaves are used in medicine. The drug is considered to be tonic and astringent for treatment of diarrhoea. It is also prescribed for rheumatism, epilepsy, general debility, and cancerous sores.

6. Ch'ing-hsiang. *Celosia argentea*

    This is a weed which grows among field crops. It is consumed by the Chinese both as food and medicine. The bruised stalk and leaves are applied as a poultice in the treatment of infected sores, wounds, and skin eruptions. The juice is taken internally for pestilential difficulties. The seeds, applied for infections of the eyes, are considered to be cooling, anti-scorbutic or anti-scurvy, and tonic.

7. Tzu-tsao. *Lithospermum officinale*. Groomwell

    This herb is indigenous to the central and northern provinces of China. The root is used as dye and medicine. Medicinally, the root is believed helpful to the blood and to the skin and all passages of the body, particularly the intestinal canal and urinary tract. The herb is also used for skin infections and eruptive fevers.

Herbs Used Especially in the Treatment of Female Ailments:

1. Ta-chi. *Euphorbia pekinensis*

    A common marsh plant with a hollow stem. It is poisonous and has a bitter taste. Although the acrid juice from the stem supposedly cures toothache, the root of the plant is a main ingredient in Chinese medicine. Ta-chi is believed to quiet the uterus during pregnancy. It also is a favorite remedy for persistent nausea and vomiting in pregnancy, as well as bowel and kidney ailments.

2. Shu-ti-huang. *Rehmania glutinosa*

   This plant has hairy leaves and scapes, red and yellow flowers, capsulated fruits, small greyish-brown seeds, and large, juicy roots. Shu-ti-huang is made from the juicy roots after repeating the processes of steaming and drying nine times. It is considered a tonic which harmonizes, increases, and cools the blood, strengthening the marrow. The drug is used in diseases of pregnancy, puerperal difficulties, and in diseases of children. It is also recommended for all wasting diseases and weakened conditions of the body.

3. Chuan-pei-mu. *Fritillaria roylei*. Fritillary, Caladium

   The plant is lilaceous and has yellow or grayish-white flowers. The starchy corns are used in medicine. They are prescribed for deficiency of milk, threatened mammary abscesses, and lingering labor. They are also used for diseases of the eye, bowels, and bone marrow; and can be applied to spider, snake, and scorpion bites.

4. Tze-lan. *Arethusa japonica*

   This small plant belongs to the order of chrysanthemum. It has purplish-black roots and bears purplish-red flowers. The leaves and stem are used in medicine. This herb is considered indispensable for the treatment of diseases related to pregnancy. It is also used to treat abscesses and diseases of the bowels.

5. Ti-fu-tzu. *Kochia scoparia*. Summer Cypress

   This plant grows in marshes, fields, and gardens. The seeds, shoots, and leaves are all used in medicine. They are all attributed with diuretic and restorative properties. The seeds are used for incontinence of urine in pregnant women, fevers, colds, and dysentery. The shoots and leaves are used for dysentery, diarrhoea, and digestive ailments.

6. Lien fang. *Nelumbium speciosum*

   This plant grows in stagnant ponds. Different parts of the plant are thought to purify the body of noxious poisons and evil conditions. Medicinally, it is antihemorrhagic, nutrient, and tonic. It is prescribed to promote the expulsion of the placenta, and to counteract the poison of deleterious fungi.

7. Tan-shen. *Salvia miltiorrhiza*

   This plant has three to seven hirsute leaves and large violet flowers. When it is fresh, the root is red outside and purple in-

side. It tastes like licorice. This herb is always prescribed in all
blood difficulties, hemorrhages, menstrual disorders, and miscar-
riages because of its antispasmodic, tonic, sedative and alterative
properties.

**Miscellany—Herbs Used in the Treatment of a Variety of Condit-
tions and Illnesses:**

1. Pei-ma-tzu. *Ricinus communis.* Castor Bean
    This is a fast-growing plant with two varieties, red-stemmed
    and white-stemmed. The seeds are used in Chinese medicine. In-
    ternally, they are used to treat scrofula, diarrhoea, debility,
    dyspepsia. Externally, the seeds are used to treat abscesses.
2. Li-lu. *Veratrum.* Mountain Onion
    This plant appears to be embraced by bundles of hairy fibers. It
    has some poisonous properties. It is used to clean nasal passages,
    as an emetic, expectorant, and evacuant. Li-lu is employed mainly
    as an emetic to treat apoplexy. It is also applied as an ointment to
    itches and parasitic skin diseases.
3. Ku-shen. *Sophora angustifolia*
    This plant with yellowish-white flowers is common in Central
    China. Its large, yellowish root has an extremely bitter taste. The
    root is prescribed for fevers, jaundice, dysentery, leprosy,
    scrofula, and many other illnesses. Although the root is used most
    in medicine, the fruits are also considered restorative and tonic.
4. Chih-mu. *Anemarhena asphodeloides*
    This is a liliaceous plant. The drug is irregular, flattened,
    twisted, and shrivelled in appearance. It is bitter to taste. The rhi-
    zome has cooling, soothing, expectorant, and diuretic properties.
5. Tien-kua-ti. *Cucumis melo*
    The Latin name refers to the cucumber-like and egg-shaped
    fruit of cucurbitaceous plants. The Chinese regarded these melons
    as deleterious. Medicinally, the stalks are recommended for in-
    testinal parasites, indigestion, jaundice, and acute colds.
6. Mu-chin-pi. *Hibiscus syriacus.* Shrubby Althea
    This plant bears red flowers that look like Althea rose. The
    bark and roots are used in medicine for treating diarrhoea,
    dysentery, dysmenorrhoea, and itchy skin diseases.
7. Pi-hsiao. Tannin
    This is a yellowish, astringent substance derived from oak bark

and gallnuts. It is prescribed to relieve constipation, indigestion, fever, and dysmenorrhoea.

8. Ho-shih. *Carpesium abrotanoides*
   The plant's leaves resemble cabbage and it bears small, yellow flowers. The seeds (Ho-shih) are slightly poisonous with a pungent, bitter taste. The leaves, roots, and seeds are all used in medicine. In addition to treating bronchial diseases, it is used to treat spitting of blood and mucus from the lungs and for ague. It is prescribed as an astringent, diuretic, expectorant, and anti-worm agent.

9. Koan-tung-hua. *Petasites japonicus*
   This plant is in the order of chrysanthemum. The flower buds are used in medicine for their expectorant, digestive, purulent, peptic, disinfectant properties. It is used to suppress coughs.

10. Pian-shui
    This plant resembles the polygonum. The leaves and stems are used in medicine. They are recommended for jaundice, kidney stones, cholera, worms, diuresis, and abdominal pain.

11. Tsao-chio-tzu. *Gleditschia japonica*
    This leguminous tree bears a pod which contains flat, brown seeds. Medicinally, the pods are considered to be an expectorant, emetic, and purgative. They are given in coughs, flatulence, chronic dysentery, and prolapsed rectum. The seeds and pods are sometimes used as an antidote to metallic poisoning.

12. Chi-ke. *Hovenia dulcis*. Japanese Raisin Tree
    This tree yields small, dry, and pea-like fruits. The fruits and stalks are considered laxative, diuretic, and quieting to the stomach. The bark is prescribed for rectum diseases.

13. Fei-tsao-tzu. *Gymnocladus chinensis*
    The seeds of this plant are black and smooth. This herb is used for rheumatism, dysentery, eczema, and venereal sores.

14. Kan-sui. *Euphorbia sieboldiana*
    This is a common weed found in central China. The ginger-like root has a reddish skin and white flesh. It is generally prescribed for abdominal swelling and hernia. Externally, Kan-sui is often applied to aching parts of the body to relieve pain and numbness.

15. Chu-ju. *Bambusa, Phyllostachys*. Bamboo
    Chu-ju is the thin outside skin of the bamboo. It is considered a

sedative, cooling to the blood, and a relief for coughs and vomiting.

16. Tien-ma. *Gastrodia elata*

This orchid-like plant has large potato-like roots with twelve small tubers on the sides. The tubers are used for food and medicine. The herb expels all kinds of effluvia, gives strength to the body, improves the circulation, and strengthens the memory. It is given for rheumatism, neuralgia, paralysis, lumbago, and headaches, and is believed to be a tonic and aphrodisiac.

17. Fang-chi. *Cocculus*

This brown, bulky, and tuberous root has a bitter taste. It is considered to be a diuretic and is prescribed for fevers, swelling, rheumatism, and pulmonary diseases. The fruits are also used for prolapsed rectum.

18. Feng-hsien-hua. *Impatiens balsamina*

This plant is insect free. It bears red, purple, and white flowers which are used in medicine for their cooling muscilaginous properties. They are used to treat snake bites, lumbago and to improve circulation and coagulation of the blood.

19. She-ch'uang-tzu. *Cnidium monneri*. Selinum Japonicus Seed

This is a fragrant plant. The seeds are used in medicine. In addition to its special effects on the kidneys, the drug is thought to be aphrodisiac, astringent, and sedative. The powdered seeds are prescribed for prolapsed rectum, piles, leprous and scabious sores.

20. Fang-feng. *Siler divaricatum*

The roots, leaves, flowers, and seeds are all used in medicine. The root, similar to the carrot, has a sweet, aromatic taste. It is given for all ailments due to damp and chill, circulatory diseases, general debility, and aconite poisoning. The leaves are prescribed for fevers. The flowers are used in circulatory disturbance and the seeds for obstinate colds.

21. Tsang-shu. *Atradylis ovata*

This plant looks like ginger. It has a bitter taste and aromatic smell. It is a favorite cure for fevers, flu, chronic dysentery, general swelling, rheumatism, profuse sweating and apoplexy.

22. Chang-shan. *Orixa japonica, Dichroa febrifuga*

This plant is less than four feet high and has a round, pointed stalk with opposite leaves shaped like the tea-leaf. The leaves, shoot, stalk, and roots are all used in medicine. The herb is considered poisonous and is used in fevers, particularly those of malarial origin, and for goiter.

23. Ju-hsiang. *Boswellia*

This herb is pale yellow, opaque, and oval. It has a bitter, aromatic taste and smells like balsam. The inferior kind is used by the Chinese for incense. The herb has sedative, tonic, stimulant, alterative, astringent, and diuretic properties. Plasters and salves to dress boils and chronic sores are made from this herb. Internally, it is prescribed for leprosy, goiter, and bladder and urinary tract disorders.

24. Shih-liu-pi. *Punica granatum*. Pomegranate Bark

There are red, yellow, and white-flowered plants under this name. Each bears sweet, sour, and bitter fruits, respectively. The peel of each has astringent properties. It is given in dysentery, seminal losses, paralysis, and for intestinal worms.

25. Huang-ching. *Polygonatum giganteum*. Solomon's Seal

This is a plant growing in the mountains whose leaves resemble those of the bamboo. The root is used in medicine more than other parts of the plant. The root is either steeped in wine or administered in powder. Its properties are tonic, constructive, and prophylactic. The herb is recommended for the treatment of confirmed leprosy.

26. Mien-hua-tzu. *Gossypium herbaceum*

These are seeds from the cotton plant. Medicinally, they are recommended as a demulcent for leprosy, scabies, and other skin diseases. The Chinese also use cotton-seed oil for cooking and light.

27. Tzu-chin-pi. *Cercis chinensis*

This is the Juadas tree of Red bud. It bears purple flowers. The wood and bark are used in medicine. They are given for bladder disease, rabies, intestinal parasites of all kinds, severe post-partum discharges, and bleeding hemorrhoids.

28. Mi-meng-hua. *Buddleja officinalis maximonwioz*

This is a shrub of the natural order Scrophularineae, which bears purple flowers. The flowers are used in medicine. The herb is used exclusively to treat various eye diseases.

29. Shih-chun-tzu. *Quisqualis indica*

This is a climbing vine that grows on trees or poles. Its leaves resemble those of Acantho-panax. The seeds are used for medicine. They are considered a safe and efficient vermifuge for children, especially worms that cause marasmus wasting, disease, and enlarged abdomen. This herb is also prescribed for children's diarrhoea. Macerated in oil, it can be used to treat parasitic skin diseases.

30. Ma-huang-ken. *Ephedra vulgaris.* Shrubby Root

This leafless plant slightly resembles equisetum. It bears yellow flowers and red, edible berries. The stems, joints, and roots are used in medicine. The stems are given for fevers, especially malarial fevers, coughs, influenza, and post-partum problems. The roots and joints have properties directly opposite to those of the stems. They are prescribed only in profuse sweating.

Ing Hay, about 1887, shortly before or after his arrival in the United States. He is dressed in traditional Chinese clothing.

Lung On, about 1878. The cap and clothing show him as a young scholar. The books are copies of the Chinese classics. The pipe is a water pipe used to smoke tobacco. This picture was probably taken in Canton, China.

John Day, around 1860. Note hoses for hydraulic mining at center and sluice box in foreground.

John Day, 1910. Chinatown is between the river and the tall trees. The Kam Wah Chung Building is visible between the tallest of the trees and the two-story schoolhouse.

Chinatown, John Day, 1909. The automobile in front of the Kam Wah Chung Building was probably Lung On's. The community temple (Joss House) is the flat-roofed building to the right and rear of the car.

Kam Wah Chung restored to its 1940 appearance, on its original site near the John Day City Park.

Doc Lee, who taught herbal medicine to Ing Hay. This picture was probably taken in the 1870's. Note the traditional shaved forehead.

Unidentified man known as "the meanest man in Chinatown." Some people believed he was from Jacksonville in Southern Oregon, and was a member of a rival tong.

Old Man Howe, a Chinese laundryman in John Day, about 1900.

Two Chinese residents of John Day, identified as Mr. Tung and Mr. Hang. The picture was taken somewhere between 1900 and 1910.

Doctor Hay and Lung On with two unidentified lady friends from the John Day area.

Doctor Ing Hay and friend, Mrs. Truesdell, on the porch of the Kam Wah Chung Building in the 1930's.

Ing Hay in old age, around 1950. He was completely blind by this time.

Portrait of Lung On in middle age, probably between 1920 and 1930.

Lung On, on the streets of John Day, about 1940.

Lung On's friend, Markee Tom, known as the "Oriental Barbarian," posing with his buckaroo friends.

"Herb Cage" in the Kam Wah Chung Building. This is where Ing Hay prepared his medicines. Boxes on shelves, left, contain medical herbs. During the Gold Rush, gold dust was weighed in this locked and barred cage.

The kitchen of the Kam Wah Chung Building. Note the altar to the Kitchen God behind the wood stove. Ing Hay brewed his herbs on this stove. The Kam Wah Chung Building was the center of social life for the Chinese in John Day.

The shrine where Doc Hay made daily offerings to his traditional gods is in the upper left corner.

Here Lung On sold notions and dry goods. A secret cache of bootleg liquor was found under the floor beneath the table.

Doc Hay's bedroom. This is the one room in the Kam Wah Chung Building that has not been restored. Damage to wallpaper occurred long after Ing Hay's death.

The storeroom of Kam Wah Chung. Products pictured came from China, Japan, and all over the United States.

The Authors

Jeffrey Barlow and Christine Richardson are a husband-wife team of historians interested in Asia and Asian immigrant communities. They were the co-directors of the Kam Wah Chung Inventory Project.

Jeffrey received his Ph.D. from the University of California, Berkeley, and has taught Asian and American history at the University of California, Riverside; also the University of Oregon. He currently teaches Asian history at Lewis and Clark College in Portland. He speaks and reads Chinese and has lived in Chinese cultures in Asia for several years.

Christine is a fourth-generation Oregonian whose family has been concerned with Asia, literally for centuries. She is descended from Jason Starbuck, who reportedly brought the first chest of tea to the colonies from China. She has lived in Asia for much of her life, including considerable time in Vietnam. She has been a friend of China for many years and continues to study Chinese language and history.

Jeffrey and Christine recently returned from China and hope one day to return to visit Kwangtung, the home province of many of the Chinese who lived in Eastern Oregon.